T0348367

RESHORE

RESHORE

HOW TARIFFS WILL BRING OUR JOBS HOME + REVIVE THE AMERICAN DREAM

SPENCER MORRISON

The Calamo Press

Washington D.C.

calamopress.com

Currente-Calamo LLC

Cover design by Mike Jackson, Beck & Stone

Interior design by Kim Hall

Library of Congress Cataloging-in-Publication Data has been applied for.

Hardcover ISBN: 9781958682142

E-Book ISBN: 9781958682098

Printed in the United States of America

10   9   8   7   6   5   4   3   2   1

In Memoriam J.D. Murphy

SPENCER MORRISON

Spencer P. Morrison B.A., J.D., is a lawyer, entrepreneur, and independent intellectual, with a focus on applied philosophy, empirical history, and practical economics. He is a founding partner of Morrison LLP, practicing primarily in the areas of divorce, civil litigation, and wills and estates. He provides extensive pro bono legal services to the victims and families of trafficked children. Spencer is the Editor-in-Chief of the *National Economics Editorial*. His work on tariffs and trade policy has been featured in major publications including the BBC, *Real Clear Politics*, the *Daily Caller*, *American Greatness*, the *Western Journal*, the *American Thinker*, and the *Foundation for Economic Education*.

TABLE OF CONTENTS

PROLOGUE

I am a divorce lawyer. I deal with people at their lowest lows—a wife who was doused with battery acid by an abusive spouse; a husband who had not seen his daughter in nine months over allegations of "black magic"; a child abducted by fraudulent foster parents.

But at the root of most of the tragedies I see? Money.

Indeed, in my experience disagreements about money or financial struggles are the primary reason marriages end in divorce. A thriving economy produces wealth and provides a sense of worth for its citizens which results in happy couples and strong communities. When a community is supported by access to good-paying jobs, more people get married, more people have kids and church attendance and civic engagement are higher.

And when an economy is in the doldrums, the opposite occurs.

Which my primary motivation for writing this book.

Let me tell you an all-too-typical example from my professional experience." It is about a client named "Mike". At one point, Mike had it all: a wife, four kids, and beautiful house just outside of town. He sat on the vestry of his town's Anglican church. His kids attended the local, Christan school. His son played hockey. His daughters competed in gymnastics. He was living the fairytale middle-class life.

Mike worked at Wingham's Westcat, a manufacturing facility that made castings of exhaust manifolds and other automotive parts. Wingham's foundry first opened in 1902 making cast iron wood stoves before transitioning to automotive parts in the 1970s, selling primarily to companies like Ford, GM and Volvo.

In 2009, Westcat consolidated its two plants in Wingham into one, laying off 140 workers in the process. Four years later, Wescast was purchased

1

by Sichuan Bohong of China for $200 million, and soon after, on May 29, 2023, Westcast announced that the company's foundry would be "temporarily" closing. During the shutdown, the parts would be manufactured in Wescast's plant in Wuhan, China, and then shipped to Wingham for machining. Mike was furloughed.

Less than a year later in April of 2024, Mike was permanently laid off. During that year his marriage had deteriorated. He and his wife had frequently argued about money. He'd had to ask his in-laws for help with private school tuition. He'd had to cut back on his children's activities and on giving to his church. His entire life was turned upside down.

As I write, he and his wife are separated and she recently filed for divorce. Working two jobs, including nights at a fast-food restaurant, he is earning barely half what he did at Westcat.

Of course, it is a familiar story – that of the decline of our manufacturing base and, in microcosm, its human toll. At its peak, over 800 persons worked at Wingham. It was the lifeblood of the community. By the time the plant shut down, it employed only 300, and now they were out of work, too. The company no longer has a plant in Wingham. The plant is shuttered. The fence surrounding the plant is padlocked. The parking lot is empty with weeds taking over. Vandals have graffitied the exterior. Decay has set it.

The community's primary employer is no more and a sense of angst has set in among the locals. The local tax base is devastated.

I tell this story to emphasize that "the economy" is not a pie-in-the-sky idea. The economy is deeply personal. It impacts the health of our families and the welfare of our children. This is why you should care about the economy. And this is why I wrote this book.

Our elites say the economy is strong: unemployment is low, and wages are high—and they supposedly have the data to back this up. But it is a pack of lies.

2

America's economy is a disaster. The rate of economic growth is the slowest it's been since the Great Depression, with Americans earning less than at any time in the past half century. By the millions, our young are being robbed of their future, unable to afford to build families or buy homes.

How so? In 1973, the median home cost 3.2 times the median household income. Meaning that if a young couple saved up every penny for just over three years, they could buy a brand-new home. Today, that ratio is over 7.5. Owning a home used to be the key to the American Dream. For tens of millions, it is now a pipe dream.

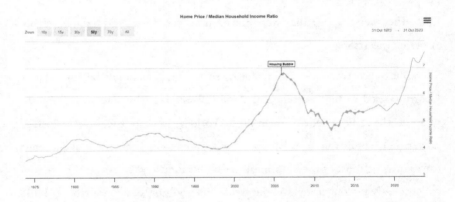

Thankfully, it is not too late. We still have time to fix the economy—but only if we find the courage to speak the truth and summon the will to act. To do this we will have to abandon deeply rooted preconceptions about how the economy works, ignore the partisan talking points we hear on the news, and understand the reality that our Founding Fathers knew all too well: that an independent nation needs an independent economy.

Look on my works, ye mighty…

In this book I will do three things. First, summarize America's economic problems. Second, show what is causing these problems. Third, explain how to fix the problems.

Here is a more detailed breakdown.

Part I explains the ways a bad economy based on financialization (making money with money) instead of a productive economy (producing physical goods and services) harms ordinary people. For although "the economy" is intangible—we cannot reach out and touch the economy any more than we can reach out and touch "society" or "history"— there is nothing that plays so vital a part in our daily lives. We interact with the economy every time we go to work, pay our taxes, or buy food at the grocery store.

A healthy economy supports a healthy society—obviously. Historically, people with good jobs raised large families, ate healthy food, and lived long lives. They were happy. They were brave. They were free. And because of this, America was strong.

But today America's manufacturing sector has been hollowed out. Manufacturing used to be the source of America's might. Our factories built the weapons the Allies needed to win both World Wars, and it was our industrial power that rebuilt war-torn Europe. Today, American industry is like a Jenga tower missing most of the bottom blocks. Our industry teeters on the brink of collapse—we no longer make enough machine tools or semiconductors to build a modern economy. We are at China's mercy.

Meanwhile the government lies about statistics as basic as the unemployment rate. They claim it is just 3.5%, when in reality it is more than twice as high. And even as wages increase, the rate of increase lags the rate of inflation, so every year it takes more money to buy less stuff.

In Part II we leave the nitty-gritty behind and view the economy from the top of the ivory tower, showing how most of America's economic problems are caused by *offshoring*—moving America's industry to foreign countries like Mexico or China.

The extent of offshoring is reflected in the size of America's trade deficit, which has increased almost every year since 1973, but accelerated dramatically after China joined the World Trade Organization in 2001. It now costs almost a *trillion* dollars every year. Once we have connected the economic dots, we will then explore how America's bad economy is at the root of our social and political problems.

The ripple effects are endless. The unemployment rate is closely connected to social problems as disparate as pornography addiction and the divorce rate. Likewise, the trade deficit is connected to just about everything, from our national security to the amount of plastic garbage floating in the ocean.

Inflation likewise affects things as basic as our diet—we simply cannot afford to eat as healthy as our grandparents did. This has had disastrous health consequences for individuals and for society. For example, the switch from animal-based fats to seed-oils are largely to blame for the epidemics of obesity, diabetes, and cancer plaguing America. It is also largely to blame for the decline in testosterone levels of American men—which harms not only millions of individual men, but the women who love them, and the country that so desperately needs them.

Part III will even more fully unmask our foe. It will show you why modern economics is not just the "dismal" science—it is a sham science. It is an ivory tower built on foundations of sand.

To begin with, we will debunk arguments in favor of global free trade. After this, we will answer the most important question in economics: how does the economy grow? In short, economic growth depends on technological growth. If we want to get rich, we first need to get smart.

Lastly, we will see how countries used protective *tariffs*—taxes on imports—to strengthen their economies -- and how high tariffs can also fix America's economy.

Although I know well that in some quarters – notably government offices and corporate boardrooms -- my argument will be unpopular, it must not fall on deaf ears. Indeed, such opposition should be seen for what it is, and filed under 'Know Your Enemies.' The sad fact is, much of the American public has been brainwashed into believing the lie that "free trade" is synonymous with *fair* trade. It is anything but. More accurately, it is profoundly *unfair* trade, benefitting only China and the Western elites who put their own interest above their nations'. It is a shameless fraud, as this book will show, deeply inimical to America's fundamental interests. We must instead embrace the sensible trade policy of our Founders, who understood the recklessness of the course on which we have so heedlessly embarked.

ALASTOR

Before we begin, I have a few housekeeping remarks.

First, this is not an academic paper designed to be read by a few dozen stuffy eggheads. Instead, this book is for the layman—especially people who do not care about economics. Therefore, I do not use many footnotes, because they often break up the book's flow and confuse casual readers.

Also, most of the data in this book is freely available from public sources. If you want to check a statistic, you can easily find it on the internet.

Second, this book is not a Franken-book, which loosely stitches together other people's ideas. Instead, it is a stream of consciousness. Thousands of books and articles, on hundreds of topics, are connected in ways that make attributing ideas a fool's errand. As such, I do not make efforts to credit historical thinkers with every idea in this book. When I do reference someone, I usually do so in the body of the text.

Third, although academics is important, I learned much of what I know through my own business and investing (mis)adventures. For example, I am a named partner at a successful law firm, I run a property holding and development company, and I was the Editor-in-Chief of the *National Economics Editorial*—a now dormant online newspaper that was viciously censored by the mainstream media a few years ago.

In short, I have practiced what I preached. I learned that knowledge is no substitute for experience. Sometimes I learned this the hard way—but what does not kill you makes you stronger—and hopefully wiser.

Fourth and finally, the government's response to Covid-19 has caused enormous economic damage—damage which has skewed the data so greatly that the last two years can safely be characterized as *outliers*. Additionally, the political climate has become so toxic, and the bureaucracy so estranged from the people, that the objectivity of certain data is now questionable. I discuss this problem in more detail when we talk about the unemployment rate an inflation. In any case, this book looks at historical trends, and therefore uses data from before 2020.

PART I

REVERE'S LAST RIDE, ON AMERICA'S ECONOMIC DECLINE

Perhaps the sentiments contained in the following pages, are not yet sufficiently
fashionable to procure them general Favor; a long Habit of not thinking
a Thing wrong, gives it a superficial appearance of being right, and
raises at first a formidable outcry in defense of Custom. But the
Tumult soon subsides. Time makes more Converts than Reason.

~ Thomas Paine, Common Sense (1775)

Thomas Jefferson. George Washington. James Madison. These names come to mind when we remember the American Revolution—and for good reason. Jefferson penned the *Declaration of Independence*. Washington defeated the British at Yorktown. Madison drafted the *Constitution*. They are America's Founding Fathers. Our cultural icons. Heroes.

The Founding Fathers were adored in life and glorified in death: we carved their faces in stone, and adorned our currency with their images. So too are the Revolution's heroes, like Paul Revere or Benjamin Franklin, immortalized in the highest art and lowest folklore—with one exception—Thomas Paine. When Paine died just six people attended his funeral, despite America owing him her very existence.

In 1775 Thomas Paine published *Common Sense*, in which he made the "for dummies" case for revolution. His work spread like wildfire, becoming the Revolution's rallying cry. The pamphlet sold over 500,000 copies within the first year, and to this day it remains the most popular work written by any American author. Why was *Common Sense* so popular?

In short: *simplicity*. Paine took lofty philosophies and summarized them in plain English—the sort of plain English that men with jobs and families— men who did not have years to waste naval-gazing—could understand. He spoke to the common man about the common good. In the end, Pain's simple words convinced more men to fight for freedom than did Jefferson's imperious logic or Franklin's obsequious rhetorical flourishes.

This book is *Common Sense* for economics.

I say this for two reasons. First, this book takes complicated economic concepts and makes them simple. After reading this book you will know *why* America's economy is bad, and *how* we can fix it.

Second—and more importantly—this book is a battle-cry. America used to be a land of opportunity. A land where parents—for perhaps the first time in human history—*knew* that their children would live in a country that was richer than the one they grew up in. That was the essence of the American Dream.

The American Dream is dead. Today our cities crumble around us, while the huddled masses search for jobs that no longer exist. Millions of good-paying factory jobs moved to Mexico and China. We are poorer today than we were yesterday—and things are only getting worse.

These facts should upset you. They should make you mad. Furious. This is a blessing. As St. Augustine said, anger can give us the energy we need to right wrongs; to fix what is broken. So long as we have anger, we have hope.

CHAPTER 1

AHAB'S OBSESSION: HUNTING AMERICA'S REAL UNEMPLOYMENT RATE

In Herman Melville's classic novel Moby Dick, the reckless Captain Ahab hunts the high seas for the legendary white whale. In doing so, he seals his own fate. In many ways our government is like Captain Ahab and the unemployment rate is the white whale.

Think about it. The government obsesses with making the unemployment rate as low as possible. All the while, it not only ignores other economic data, but will sacrifice other aspects of our economic wellbeing to reduce the unemployment rate. Not only that, but the government's obsession with a low unemployment rate has caused the government to lie to itself—and to us—just like Captain Ahab himself.

Consider that in 1992 President Bill Clinton's campaign coined the phrase "it's the economy, stupid." Since then, almost every politician—Democrats and

Republicans—parrots this talking point. All we hear on the campaign trail is talk of jobs, jobs, and more jobs.

In 1994 President Clinton touted the North American Free Trade Agreement ("NAFTA") would create "a million [new American] jobs in the first five years."[1] Two decades later, President Donald Trump won the 2016 election largely because he promised to bring back those jobs destroyed by NAFTA. In a sense, NAFTA did not really matter—what mattered is whether the public thought it created or destroyed jobs. Either way, NAFTA was the *Pequod* and our political Ahab's caught their white whales.

To make "whaling" easier the government publishes an official unemployment rate. Typically, the national unemployment rate hovers around 5%. Most people assume this means 95 out of every 100 Americans have jobs. Meanwhile, only 5 out of 100 are out of work. While this assumption seems like common sense, it could not be further from the truth. In reality, the unemployment rate is over twice what the government claims.

I am sure many of you suspected as much. We all know someone whose life has been shattered by chronic unemployment. Perhaps it is your father's, who suddenly lost his job after 30 years at the factory. Now he scrapes by on his pension, living month to month. Or it could be your friend from college. She has a master's degree but works part-time at Starbucks—there are just no full-time jobs available. Or maybe it is your son. He could not find any entry level jobs as a teenager. Now he lives in your basement gaming and vaping.

Everyone's story is slightly different, but the plot is the same: there are no jobs.

According to data from Workopolis, an online employment agency, just 2% of job applicants receive interviews. The ratio is even lower for jobs with above-average salaries.[2] Everyone knows someone who is unemployed, and yet according to the government these people simply do not exist.

They are statistically invisible. Where did they go? What is their story?

Lies, damned lies, and statistics[3]

The government's response to Covid-19 has grossly distorted America's labor market, and the recent employment data shows us little about the historical trends. It is an *outlier*—a piece of data so different from the rest that it cannot be caused by an ongoing trend. Outliers have their own unique explanations.

In this case we will ignore them and instead concentrate on the unemployment rate from September 2019—a few months before the Covid lockdowns. At that time the official unemployment rate was 3.5%. This was the lowest it had been in 20 years. Unfortunately, this statistic is a damned lie.

Our story begins with an explanation of how the Bureau of Labor Statistics ("BLS") calculates America's unemployment rate. They begin by estimating America's total population. At the time America was home to roughly 328,300,000 people.

Next, they subtract the *institutional population* from the total population. This is a fancy term for people who the BLS deems unable to hold private sector jobs. This includes, for example, active-duty military personnel, prison inmates, wards in mental facilities, people in old folks' homes, and everyone under the age of 16. This is fair enough. After all, there are very few people who would expect a nine-year-old kiddo to hold a full-time job.

The remaining 259,638,000 people are called the *civilian noninstitutional population*. This is the government's best estimate of everyone who could potentially work. The BLS then sub-divides the civilian noninstitutional population into two more groups.

The first group is the *civilian labor force*. This includes everyone who is *employed*, currently working, and everyone who is *unemployed*, not currently working but searching for a job. There are 164,039,000 such people.

The second group is *not in labor force*. There are 95,599,000 such people. These people do not work, and according to the government, do not want jobs. We will talk about these people in more detail later in this chapter.

The official unemployment rate is simply the percentage of people in the civilian labor force who are unemployed. As of September 2019, there were 5,769,000 unemployed people. Thus, the unemployment rate was 3.5%. All of this is relatively straightforward. The real question is, where are all the missing people? It turns out that they are hiding in plain sight.

The key to reconciling the paradox between the job market we see, and the story the government sells, is how the BLS defines *unemployment*. A person is considered employed if they do any sort of work, for any sort of pay or profit. This not only includes people with full time jobs, but also people with part-time jobs. Even if you work just one hour per week, you are considered fully employed for the government's purposes.

This is already misleading. Most people would not consider themselves "working" if they usher at a movie theatre every Friday night. Perhaps more importantly, society in general would not consider them "employed" in the common sense of the word. Think about it: if you had to describe someone in this position to a friend, would you say they were gainfully employed at the movie theatre, or would you call them a bum who makes a few bucks every Friday at the movies?

To further complicate things: the BLS can "deem" that you earn a profit from your work—even if you were not paid. That is, they can just make stuff up. For example, a 16-year-old who helps on his family farm is considered employed, as if he worked at a grocery store. Likewise, a stay-at-home mom who helps her husband with his business on the weekends is also considered fully employed. Because of this, you can be fully employed without ever earning a single dollar. So much for common sense.

These loosey-goosey classifications fudge the numbers, and the government uses them the support a false narrative that unemployment is at a 20-year low. Remember, although 158,269,000 are employed, just 128,436,000 of them work full time. This means that 29,833,000 people work part-time jobs.

There is little doubt that millions of these people would prefer to work full time—if only jobs were available. Based on survey data, we know that 4,350,000 people said they were working part-time for "economic reasons"—which is code for "the economy is bad". Another 1,322,000 said they worked part-time because they admitted could not find full-time positions.

On top of this, 2,588,000 Americans said they worked part-time due to slack work protocols. This is when a company "temporarily" reduces its business when there is little or no work available. These employees are not actually working, but they are counted as employed because they have employment contracts, and are theoretically still on payroll. That said, there is no guarantee that they will be called back to work, nor that they will return to full-time hours when they do.

These 8,260,000 Americans are *visibly underemployed*. That is, they are not working at their full capacity because of economic factors beyond their control—there are no jobs, or they have a job on paper, but there is no work for them to do so they have been put on a shelf for later.

This is an enormous number of people—a huge amount of wasted talent. And yet, the plight of these people is not reported by the mainstream media, or addressed by politicians. They have been written out of America's economic story.

THE INVISIBLE MAN

Another big problem with the employment rate is that it tells us nothing about people who are *underemployed*. That is, people who are highly qualified or experienced, but unable to find work in their field, or work otherwise commensurate with their qualifications.

We have all heard the joke about Starbucks baristas with a PhD in gendered basket-weaving, but underemployment is no joke. Many people do everything "right"—they have STEM degrees or trade school diplomas—but cannot find work because there is *no* work.

For example, during my undergraduate degree I worked part time at a bookstore. One of my coworkers had a PhD in organic chemistry. She designed and fabricated a unique molecule for her thesis. I asked her why she was working as an entry level employee. She gave me two reasons. First, she could not find a job as a chemist—despite all the hype surrounding STEM degrees. Second, she could not find a better job because she was always "overqualified".

Although this is anecdotal evidence—it is based on my own experience and observations—it is the best we have. There is simply no way to objectively measure whether employees are overqualified for their current jobs, other than to ask them. A few surveys did just that.

In 2011 Randstad, an international human resources company, conducted a large-scale survey of American workers. In total, 33% of Americans reported that they were overqualified for their jobs.[4] This number has only increased. Prior to Covid-19, over 48% of college graduates indicated that they were underemployed.

A 2017 study conducted by Stephen J. Rose attempted to objectively examine whether workers with Bachelor of Art's ("BA") degrees were underemployed in their profession. Rose considered various metrics like whether their degree's skills were likely to be used in their profession, and whether their degrees afforded them an earning's premium relative to workers without degrees.[5]

Rose found 25% of workers with BA's—3,603,000 people—were objectively underemployed. Although the paper did not consider students with other levels and educational backgrounds, it is plausible that these findings may be similar with graduate students.

In short, the unemployment rate is just a number. It does not tell the full story. Millions of Americans work part-time jobs—millions more only earn theoretical incomes. Nevertheless, they are fully "employed" according to the government.

Likewise, tens of millions of Americans work low-end jobs when they could be doing something far more productive. If jobs were as plentiful as the government claims, we would not see engineers driving taxis or PhDs working at bookstores.

In obsessing over the unemployment rate, our politicians have completely lost the plot.

INTO SNAEFELLSJOKULL

Not only does the government mislead the American public: it outright lies.

The BLS states that 5,769,000 are *unemployed*. Remember, to be "unemployed" these people must actively look for work. They must send job applications, resumes, and cover letters—even if they receive no reply. If not, they are no longer unemployed, they are reclassified as *not in the labor force*.

This is where the plot thickens: stop applying for jobs for four weeks? Presto. You are not unemployed. You are simply enjoying a Seinfeld-esque "summer of George"—except you probably cannot afford to eat a whole wheel of cheese like our short, stalky, bald friend.

The BLS estimates that there are some 1,299,000 people who are *marginally attached* to the labor force. In layman's terms, these are people who are looking for work but have not sent out a new resume in the four weeks preceding the survey.

The BLS also estimates that there are some 321,000 *discouraged workers*. These people have stopped applying for work because there simply are no jobs available. When we include these people, this brings the number of unemployed Americans up to 7,389,000. This increases the unemployment rate to 4.5%. Unfortunately, the tale does not end here.

In 2019, America's *labor force participation rate* was 63.2%. This is the percentage of people who were either employed or unemployed, relative to the total civilian noninstitutional population. That is, everyone who could potentially work. The other 36.8% of Americans were not in the labor force. Essentially, these people are just not in the job market, so they do not count when we talk about the unemployment rate.

Importantly, the labor force participation rate is down roughly 5% from its peak in 2000. If this rate had not declined, we would expect there to be 174,736,000 Americans in the labor force, as opposed to 164,039,000. This is a difference of 10,697,374 people—this is where the government hides the real unemployment rate. Who are these people? What are their stories?

Some of these people are marginally attached and discouraged workers. However, they make up a small fraction of the group. The most obvious potential answer to this question is that they are retirees: America's population is aging and therefore the labor force will shrink. Experts spin the story of America's "greying" population constantly—the job market is fine, just let the old folks enjoy their Caribbean cruises! Unfortunately, the real numbers tell a different story. There are two reasons for this.

First, while it is true that senior citizens make up a larger share of America's population than ever before, this increase has largely been offset by a corresponding *decrease* in the proportion of Americans who are children or youths.

As a result, the share of America's working age population—the statistically relevant cohort—has barely changed since 2000. Basically, retirees were made up by teenagers reaching the age of majority.

In fact, when labor force participation peaked in 2000, some 65.9% of Americans were of "working age". In 2019, some 65.24% of Americans were "working age". The retirement surge used to justify the declining labor force participation rate never happened. At most, we can expect that retirees explain just 1,713,000 of this difference. This still leaves 7,364,000 people unaccounted for.

Second, it is plausible that retirement has not impacted the numbers whatsoever. This is because the labor force participation rate for people between the ages of 65 and 75—the first wave of baby boomers—has increased significantly. Consider that in 2000 the labor force participation rate for this cohort was just 19.2%. In 2019, this figure increased to 26.6%. Given that there are over 30,000,000 people in this age group, the increased labor force participation more than makes up for the number of people that we would expect to retire relative to the data from 2000.

To sum up, America's aging population does not explain the drop in the labor force participation rate. Now what?

20,000 LEAGUES DEEPER

In 2015 the BLS published a comprehensive article discussing how many Americans dropped out of the labor force between 2004 and 2014.[6] Given that the labor market dynamics had not materially changed between 2014 and 2019, I believe that it is reasonable to use this older data as a starting point. The article looked at data collected from the Current Population Survey and its Annual Social and Economic Supplement.

Essentially, people who were no longer in the labor force were asked why they were not working. Their responses fell into a few main categories: retired; ill health or disabled; homecare responsibilities; pursuing education; could not find work; or various other reasons.

As I have already explained, retirement is likely not a relevant factor. Next relates to disability claimants. Between 2004 and 2014 the number of Americans claiming that they could not work because of disabilities increased by 31.4%. However, according to America's Social Security Administration, the number of Americans who actually suffer from disabilities increased by 13.6% during the same period.[7] When we take the difference between these numbers, we can see 2,229,000 people who have been squeezed out of the labor market.

The next major category relates to homecare responsibilities. Typically, this refers to families with one stay-at-home parent. According to data from Pew Research, between 2000 and 2016 the percentage of stay-at-home mothers increased by 15%, whereas the number of stay-at-home fathers increased by 43%.[8]

On its face this may look like a good thing—more parents are able to afford to stay home with their children. However, many millions of parents are staying at home because they cannot find work. In particular, 33% of stay-at-home fathers, and 6% of stay-at-home mothers, said that the inability to find work was their primary reason for staying home. This means that 617,100 fathers and 547,800 mothers are not working due to economic reasons. As a result, we can add another 1,164,900 to the real unemployment rate.

The next major reason why Americans are leaving the labor force is because they are pursuing further education. This would also be good if it were true. But it is not. In 2014, the number of teenagers, aged 16 to 19, who claimed that they could not work because of schooling increased by 31%. However, school enrollment only increased by 1% during the same period.[9]

The same is true for young adults, ages 20-24. During the same period the number of young adults claiming that they could not work because of college commitments increased by 28%, however, post-secondary enrollment only increased by 8.4% during the same period.[10]

Unless young people stopped skipping class or drinking and started studying like never before, it is safe to assume most of them stopped working because there were no jobs available. So many bright, young people are being denied their chance to make their own way in life, to learn the value of a hard day's work, to get their hands dirty at a tough job—no wonder socialist sentiment has taken hold.

Finally, approximately 1,500,000 Americans noted that they had not looked for work during the past year because there was no work available. And because they did not send out any resumes within the last year, they were not included in the marginally attached worker category that we discussed earlier. As a result, these people simply fell into the statistical void.

At this point we are ready to estimate America's real unemployment rate— before any distortion from the government's job-killing Covid-19 response. In 2019 there were 5,769,000 people where were officially unemployed. On top of this, there were 1,299,000 people who were marginally attached to the labor force, and 321,000 who were classified as discouraged workers. On top of this, there were approximately 2,229,000 who claimed disability rather than work, 1,164,900 parents who relied on their partner, and 1,500,000 Americans who did not fit into any of the above categories.

In total, I estimate that the real number of unemployed Americans is **12,283,000**. The real unemployment rate is 7.5%. This is more than double what the government claims.

This story only grows more tragic when you remember that another 8,260,000 Americans worked part time, despite searching for full time employment, and untold tens of millions are underemployed. Not only do high unemployment and underemployment rates hurt America's economy by leaving our talent at the wayside—and therefore money on the table—but this causes untold social harms that the government conveniently ignores. We will talk about those in more detail in Chapter 6.

Ultimately, just as Ahab pursued his white whale as if "possessed by all the fallen angels", our government's obsession with lowering the unemployment rate is an exercise in our economic self-destruction.

CHAPTER 2

SISYPHUS'S CURSE: WAGE STAGNATION AND PRICE INFLATION

King Sisyphus of Corinth was the most cunning man of his age. The poet Homer tells us how he managed to escape Erebus—the underworld from Greek mythology—not once but twice. As punishment for embarrassing the Olympian Gods, Zeus cursed Sisyphus to push a boulder up a steep hill for all eternity. No matter how hard Sisyphus pushed, his muscles would eventually tire, and the boulder would roll back into the depths of Erebus.

The curse of Sisyphus is no longer just a myth—it is America's reality. American workers work harder and harder while their wages decline. We push the boulder up the hill, and it rolls down again. Disturbingly, the income of American workers peaked in 1973. It has been downhill ever since.

IN PURSUIT OF DAPHNE

The primary impact of an excessively high unemployment rate is that it gives big business leverage over workers—leverage which they use to depress wages. We will consider two periods. The first is 1950 through 1973. The second is 1974 through 2019. I have chosen 1973 as the tipping point because this was the year American wages peaked.

During the first period the average unemployment rate was 4.74%. During the second period the average unemployment rate was 6.32%. To be clear, these are averages of the "official" rate published by the Bureau of Labor Statistics. In reality, the numbers are higher, especially for the more recent years. We will explore the reasons for the increase in unemployment later. For now, we will simply look at the consequences.

The main consequence is that wages for American workers have stagnated. In fact, most workers have not received a pay raise since 1973. In 1973 the median hourly wage was $4.14. Meanwhile in 2019 the median hourly wage was $19.33. [11] On its face this looks like good news—$19.33 is much higher than $4.14.

Unfortunately, this is comparing apples to oranges. Although the median wage went up in *nominal* terms, the number itself went up, it went down in *real* terms. In other words, the amount that you can buy with $19.33 today is less than what you could buy with $4.14 back in 1973.

If we want to compare apples to apples, then we need to account for *inflation*. Every year the value of our dollar decreases, in large part, because the US government prints more dollars. The more dollars in circulation, the less each dollar is worth.

Once we account for inflation, it turns out that $4.14 in 1973 is actually worth $23.84 in 2019. This means that the average worker in 1973 earned

23.3% more than the average American today—working essentially the same sort of job for the same number of hours. This is a huge difference. In fact, if you work full time then this works out to $9,020 over a year.

What could you do with an extra $9,000 every year? Probably a whole lot. If you are a family man, I expect that you could take the wife and kids on a Caribbean cruise. Not your speed? You could buy yourself a Rolex. Heck, if you are financially responsible you could even do something crazy like pay-down your credit cards, or buy stocks. The possibilities are endless.

That said, not everyone's incomes decreased. Since 1973 the economic gains have gone to the top 20% of earners, which is why economic inequality has been increasing.[i] If today's income was dispersed like it was in 1973, then the average middle-class household would earn nearly $100,000 per year, as opposed to $69,560.[ii] This is a huge difference, and it explains why we all feel like the middle class is dying—despite what the government says.

---

i Bivens et al. "Raising America's Pay", 11. In raw numbers, the top quintile incomes grew an average of 0.65% per year, while the bottom four quintile's incomes grew at an average of 0.2% per year.

ii This is not an idle fantasy. Between 1950 and 1973 the median income rose faster than inflation, meaning that they were able to buy more stuff with the median income—their lives improved. In 1950 the median wage was ~$1.40/hour, which translates into $2.58 in 1973 dollars. In 1973, the median wage was $4.14, which is 60% higher. This means that the standard of living improved dramatically during this period.

What changed was that since 1973 pay has stopped rising in tandem with productivity. Between 1948 and 1973 the average productivity of an American worker increased by 96.7%, while hourly wages increased by 91.3% (ie. if you did more work, you were paid more). However, between 1973 and 2014 productivity increased by 72%, while real wages only increased by a meager 9.2% (real wages per hour actually declined, the increase was made by working more hours). Furthermore, this trend appears to be accelerating: between 2000 and 2014 productivity increase 21.6%, while wages only raised 1.8%.

See: Bivens & Mishel, "Understanding the Historic Divergence Between Productivity and a Typical Worker's Pay," 3.

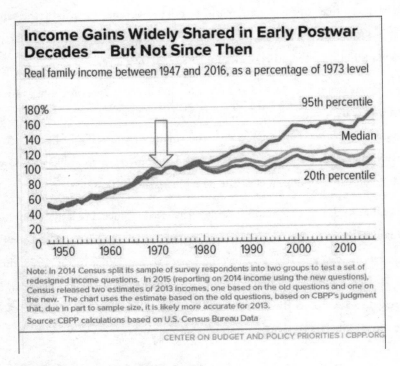

Income Gains Widely Shared in Early Postwar Decades — But Not Since Then

Real family income between 1947 and 2016, as a percentage of 1973 level

Note: In 2014 Census split its sample of survey respondents into two groups to test a set of redesigned income questions. In 2015 (reporting on 2014 income using the new questions), Census released two estimates of 2013 incomes, one based on the old questions and one on the new. The chart uses the estimate based on the old questions, based on CBPP's judgment that, due in part to sample size, it is likely more accurate for 2013.

Source: CBPP calculations based on U.S. Census Bureau Data

CENTER ON BUDGET AND POLICY PRIORITIES I CBPP.ORG

A LAMENT FOR ICARUS

"Wage stagnation" is an amorphous concept. In this section we will make it more concrete by discussing the ways it affects the daily lives of ordinary people. But first we must get back to basics and clarify some definitions. There is a difference between *needs* and *wants*. Needs are those goods and services that people *must* buy. They are not optional. Classic examples of needs include food, clothing, and shelter.

Wants are those goods and services that people choose to buy, because doing so improves their lives. Examples of wants include entertainment or vacations, non-emergency medical procedures, and education.

Most economists—and people with any common sense—recognize that a society's affluence can be measured by how much it spends on needs relative to wants. If people spend most of their income on needs, the economy is probably in bad shape because they cannot afford life's luxuries. Conversely, an affluent population will be able to spend more of their income on wants.

Economics is a tool to enrich society. As such, our economic policies should be focused on increasing the amount that we can spend on wants, without sacrificing our needs. There are two ways to do this. First, we can increase our total income. Second, we can lower the price of our needs, so that we can spend more on wants.

As we have already seen, the average American actually earns *less* today than they did in 1973. This means that the only way today's families can increase their quality of life is by spending a greater proportion of their income on wants. Unfortunately, this proportion has likewise stagnated for the last 40 years.

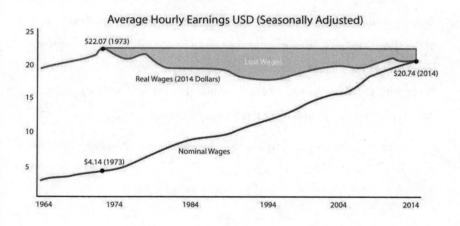

Historically, this was not the norm. Up until 1973 ordinary families were able spend more and more of their incomes on wants. For example, in 1901 families were able to spend just 20.2% of their income on life's frills and trivialities. Most of their income went to paying rent and buying groceries. By 1985 families were able to spend 48.6% of their income on wants. Over time,

Americans became richer and more decadent. This is what economic growth is all about.[12]

This pattern reversed in the 1980s. If we look at the median household spending patterns, we find that today's families are spending more on needs than they did in the 1980s. In fact, the median American household now spends just 36.7% of its expenditures on wants. This is the lowest proportion seen since the 1960s.

Many have "explained away" this phenomenon by pointing out that families are smaller today than they used to be. Therefore, it makes sense that a single individual will spend a larger share of their income on rent than will a dua

l income household. This is true. However, this logic cuts both ways.

Remember, we are talking about families. Americans had more children in the 1980s, and we would therefore expect them to spend more of their income on food and clothing. This was not the case. On top of that, people were more likely to live in single income households—dad worked, and mom stayed at home with the kids. As such, we can surmise that the economic stagnation and decline that we are witnessing is not a trick of the light. It is real.

American families are poorer today than they were yesterday. We all know it. Now we have the data to prove it.

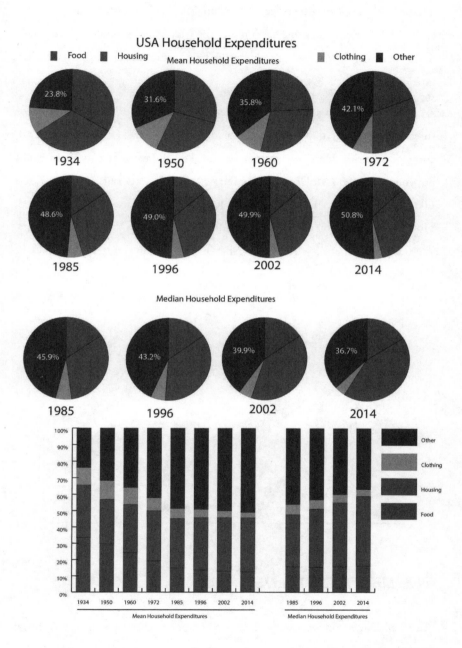

USA Household Expenditures

Economists have a running gag where they claim the best way to measure inflation is to compare the price of McDonald's Big Macs over time. Accordingly, *The Economist* magazine has run the "Big Mac Index" since 1986. Although somewhat tongue-in-cheek, the metric is helpful because it helps us visualize how inflation affects our daily lives.

To hammer this point home, we will compare the historical prices of three different everyday goods: McDonald's hamburgers, 1L bottles of Pepsi, and standard 50g Hershey candy bars. In 1985 the median household could buy roughly 19,000 McDonald's hamburgers, 12,000 bottles of Pepsi, or 27,500 Hershey candy bars with their disposable income—if that was all they wanted. However, in 2019, you could only buy roughly 11,500 McDonald's hamburgers, 7,500 bottles of Pepsi, or 15,000 Hershey Bars.[13] We live in truly dark days.

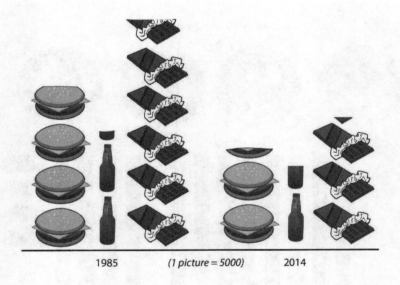

1985   *(1 picture = 5000)*   2014

THE DEATH OF TALOS

Although American wages have increased on paper, they have increased slower than the cost of living. As a result, Americans are poorer today than they were yesterday. This is an example of *visible inflation*. To complicate matters, there is also something that we will term *invisible inflation*. This type of inflation is actually more dangerous because it flies under the radar.

Invisible inflation occurs in two ways. First, when the *quality* of goods or services decreases, but the price stays the same. The decline in quality of household appliances is a good example of this. Second, invisible inflation occurs when consumers *substitute* high quality products with low quality products. The most historically relevant substitution was the shift from animal to plant-based food.

The first type of invisible inflation—when a product's quality decreases without a corresponding decrease in price—is exemplified by household appliances.[14] I have chosen household appliances because they are among the biggest purchases ordinary families make, and therefore price changes are very noticeable.

Also, appliances are manufactured goods. This means their price is less impacted by government subsidies, which artificially depress the prices of agricultural products like corn, fruit, and sugar. Finally, appliance technology has not materially changed in decades—a dishwasher from 1970 will clean your dishes just as well as one made in 2019. This makes apples-to-apples comparisons easier.

In 1976 an ordinary clothes dryer had a price tag of $291, and a typical washing machine cost $199. After adjusting for inflation, we find that that those same products would cost $1,317 and $901 in 2019. In contrast, comparable mid-range washers and dryers cost roughly $500 each in 2019.[15] The story is the same for dishwashers. In 1980 a standard dishwasher cost $249. Adjusted for inflation this works out to $809 in 2019. Meanwhile, a basic dishwasher costs approximately $500 today.[16]

On its face, it looks like the cost of household appliances has actually decreased—and this would be true were it not for *invisible inflation*.

They "don't build 'em like they used to". Yes, modern appliances have fancy bells and whistles—some even have little computer screens so they must be high-tech. However, none of that matters if the appliances are not built to last. According to estimates from Sears, modern appliances typically have service lives of 10 to 13 years, depending upon the make and model.[17] Unfortunately, most do not make it that long.

According to a survey from *Consumer Reports*, nearly one-in-three side-by-side refrigerators broke within four years. Likewise, some one-in-four washing machines, and one-in-five dishwashers failed during the same period.[18] This is in stark contract to the service life of older products, which typically lasted 25 to 30 years, and generally did not need servicing until the 15-year mark.[19]

The decrease in quality is reflected in the manufacture's reluctance to stand by their products. In the 1970s and 1980s, appliances were generally under warranty for ten years. These days, manufacturers warranties last one to two years—unless you pay extra for an extended warranty. Even then, the extended warranty usually lasts no more than five years.[20]

The reason for this is that manufacturers tailer their warranties to the expected service life of products—if they know that a warranty is not likely to cost them money until it expires, they are more than happy to advertise anything less than that as a warranty period. As such, a company offering a ten-year warranty does not actually expect to incur any significant costs until *after* the warranty expires. The same logic applies to a two-year warranty.

The opposite is also true: we can expect problems will occur only after the warranty period expires. Given the convergence of both the survey and the warranty data, we can safely assume that older household appliances lasted roughly two to three times longer than modern appliances. This means that modern appliances are not actually cheaper. Why? You have to buy them over and over again!

This begs the question: if technology has improved then why do household appliances have shorter lifespans? The answer: invisible inflation. Companies have kept nominal costs—the sticker price—down on appliances by moving their factories to China or Mexico.

They have also substituted relatively expensive, but sturdy, manufacturing processes, with cheaper, but more flimsy processes. For example, most switches and doors are now glued, as opposed to screwed, together. This causes parts of the appliances to warp and split. This leads to increased wear-and-tear, and can allow humidity to rust-away key components. Ultimately, machines fail earlier than they used to.

Another example is of the motors powering most appliances. In the past motors were made in America. Today, they are usually made in China—even if the product is "assembled" in America. In terms of manufacturing processes, components were usually die-cast, and if they were expected to be exposed to humidity, they were dipped in thick coats of paint. This created to sturdy machinery which was not likely to rust.

Today, components are usually milled, and are often made from plastic, which is flimsier than metal. When metal is used, it is generally spraypainted. This results in a thinner coat of paint, and may not protect every nook and cranny from humidity. As a result, today's machinery is more vulnerable to both wear-and-tear and rust. Overall, invisible inflation has eroded any value in having "cheaper" household appliances—and just about every other good that Americans buy.

BEING KRONOS, OR HOW TO SWALLOW STONES

The second type of invisible inflation happens when consumers substitute good quality products for bad quality products. Nowhere is this more obvious than in

America's switch from animal-based to plant-based foods. But before we can entertain this discussion, I need to explain how the government calculates inflation.

The most popular way of measuring inflation is with reference to the Consumer Price Index ("CPI"). The CPI is calculated every month by the Bureau of Labor Statistics, who tracks the change in market prices between goods and services every month. The CPI decides which goods and services are included in the CPI with reference to overall consumer spending habits, and weights the CPI accordingly.

For example, if Americans *only* bought apples, and the price of apples rose by 10%, then the inflation rate would be 10%. However, the Americans bought both apples and oranges in equal amounts, and the price of oranges did not rise, then the overall inflation rate would be 5%. Now pretend that Americans buy three times as many apples as oranges. In this case, the CPI would weight apples more heavily than oranges, and the inflation rate would be 7.5%. This CPI is basically just a more complicated version of this logic. What you need to know is that price of goods rises, so does inflation.

There are many problems with the CPI, but the biggest problem is how the CPI hides the true inflation rate by substituting expensive stuff for cheap "alternatives".[iii] As we saw earlier, the proportion of their disposable income that the typical American family spends on food has remained fairly consistent since the 1970s. Based on this data, it appears reasonable to assume that price

---

iii The CPI has many problems. Chief among them is that the CPI is not measured in reference to an objective unit. Instead, the representative basket is always changing—the goods which are included are never the same, and neither is their weight. Further, many goods—in particular new products—are left out. This means that any measurements are constantly in flux, and are of little value. This is especially true when talking about long time horizons. A good analogy is that of distance measurements: height is measured in reference to a definable unit. We know exactly how long a foot is, and therefore can compare the heights of people using an objective standard. Imagine if the length of a foot changed every month—would measuring height in feet make any sense? This is essentially what we are doing when we measure the inflation rate.

Another major problem with the CPI is that it does not adequately account for the change in quality of goods—the first type of invisible inflation. Technology can greatly increase the value of goods relative to their price. A good example of this is with iPods: iPods originally had minimal storage, and now they have evolved into powerful handheld computers. So too can poor business practices greatly decrease the value of goods relative to their price, as was the case with household appliances.

This is why I have tried to focus my analysis in this book on price changes of particular goods which can be more easily compared, such as the costs of shelter or clothing, household appliances, or meat. I have also looked at spending ratios between needs and wants, which paint a more accurate picture across long time horizons.

of food has not increased much since then—at least not relative to what people earn. This is false.

Consider that between 1970 and 2014, America's per capita consumption of red meat declined by 28%, whole milk by 79%, eggs by 13%, animal fats (like lard) by 27%, and butter by 9%. During the same period the consumption of vegetable oils increased by 87%, while the consumption of grains increased by 28%. Overall, dietary calories from animal foods declined by 21%, and calories from plants increased by 14%.[21]

Not only have the proportions of red meat decreased, but the overall amount of red meat has decreased. It is estimated that in the 1880s the average American consumed 175 lbs of meat per year—mostly red meat. Today, the average American consumes just 100 lbs of meat per year, and over half of this is less-nutritious poultry.

Essentially, American consumers have stopped buying as much meat as they used to. Instead, they eat more processed foods and vegetable fats, which are much cheaper and serve overlapping dietary functions. Basically, they swapped butter for margarine, lard for canola oil, and steaks for chicken breasts. As a result, the price of food does not appear to have increased relative to our incomes. But in reality, Americans today could simply not afford to eat the types of meals that they did in the 1970s. This sort of inflation is invisible to casual observer, and yet it has both disastrous consequences of America's quality of life and—as we shall see in Chapter 6—their physical health.

INTO THE HOUSE OF ATREUS

Since the 1980s Americans have spent more and more on needs, and less and less on wants. The biggest culprit in this pattern is that the rising price of shelter—whether rents or mortgages. Not only have prices increased, but housing is also subject to invisible inflation.

To begin with, it is worth mentioning that home ownership is not just an economic issue—the ability for any hardworking person to save enough money to buy a house has always been a part of the American Dream. Our ancestors who settled the forests of Massachusetts and Virginian mountains, and who crossed the Great Plains in covered wagons were not serfs. They were home-steaders—free men who owned their own land. Ever since, Americans have been a nation of homeowners.

This has had massive benefits to our nation. Why? Homeowners move less and invest more of their money in their property. This gives them a large personal and financial stake in their community. From this flows larger families, more respect for private property, and more tight-knit communities. Unfortu-nately, this central pillar of the American Dream is collapsing.

Today, home ownership is becoming a pipe dream for many Americans—particularly millennials. In fact, houses are at least 95% more expensive today than they were in 1973. This number already accounts for official inflation figures. According to the US Census Bureau, the median household income was $9,265 in 1973.[22]

Although this may not sound like much on paper, it was worth a lot in real terms, especially when you consider that the median sales price of a new home, as of January 1973, was just $29,900—3.2 times the median household income.[23] In other words, if the median American family saved up every penny that they earned, and put it towards a new house, it would take them just over 3 years to fully pay-off their brand new house.

House prices held steady, relative to income, for the next decade. In 1985 new home prices crept up a bit, to 3.7 times the median family income. However, during the 1990s and 2000s housing prices skyrocketed relative to wages. For example, in 2023 the median new home price was $387,600. Meanwhile, the median household income was $67,521. As a result, houses are 95% more expensive than they were in 1973.

The price of housing is yet another problem that tariffs will help address. In short -we will address in depth later in this book - we export our wealth to our foreign adversaries -such as China- through our trade deficit. Many of these foreigners then reinvest this money in U.S. real estate and Wall Street real estate investment funds. Wall Street banks then use this money (in addition to money acquired from cheap capital provided by the Federal Reserve's quantitative easing), to buy U.S. real estate and single-family homes. One study shows Wall Street will own as much as 40% of all single-family homes by 2030. And if this isn't troubling enough, invisible inflation makes this problem even worse.

Typically, one does not just buy a house. They also buy the land in what is called *fee simple*. This means that they own the land itself—including everything below and everything above. Oftentimes the land itself is the primary driver of value in a home. Case in point is the fact that infill developers will often pay above market rates to buy a property, demolish the house, and either subdivide the lot or build a new home. This is because humans have the ability to make more of just about anything—anything except new land. As a result, it is important that we compare the amount of land that sit under our houses. As it turns out, today's new homes sit on smaller lots than at any other point in recent history.

The US Census Bureau began tracking the median lot size of new home sales in 1976. During that year, the average lot was 10,125 square feet. In 2019 this number had plummeted to just 8,177 square feet—the smallest lot size on record. This is a drop of 24%. If this is added to the increase in price of the visible inflation, then we find that the price of new houses has increased by some 73% relative to the median American income.

It is also worth mentioning that the average size of new homes has increased since 1973. This is a small consolation prize, and is somewhat akin to filling up on bread at a restaurant—would you go back to a restaurant that had excellent bread, but which served tiny steaks for the same price as the restaurant down the street? Of course not.

The same is true of houses: the land is the main course, the house can be renovated, torn down and rebuilt, or demolished entirely without voiding the land's value. In any case, although houses may be superficially larger, their quality is also worse. This should be obvious to anyone, but here two important examples.

First, older homes used to be built with copper plumbing. Copper has two qualities which make it uniquely well suited for plumbing. To begin with, copper has one of the highest thermal conductivities of any material, which means you do not need to wait 5 minutes for the "hot" water to actually become hot.

Not only that, but copper is also naturally anti-bacterial, anti-viral, and is an essential trace mineral required by the human body—a trace mineral that Americans are becoming increasingly deficient in. As such, people living in houses with copper plumbing are healthier.

Next, modern construction materials are lower quality. Old houses were built and framed with wood. Today's houses are often framed with wood composites and plastics. A Latvian experiment from 2017 showed the difference between old materials, and modern "fire retardant" materials when it comes to fires.[24]

They built two houses. One was built of wood and furnished with traditional products. The second was built using fire-retardant materials and furnished with fire-retardant goods. Two tons of weight were balanced on the roofs of both houses. Both were set on fire with one candle. The experiment highlighted some very interesting findings.

First, the fire in the modern fire-retardant house burned significantly hotter, and lost its structural integrity much faster. After 7 minutes and 17 seconds the plastic-framed windows in the fire-retardant house melted, and the glass fell out. As a result, much more air was able to reach the fire. This contributed to the fire burning significantly hotter in the fire-retardant house.

Overall, the house lost its structural integrity after 36: minutes and 38 seconds. Meanwhile, the wooden house was still structurally sound after the fire was extinguished at the experiments' conclusion. This is because wood is a natural material which is already fire-retardant, in that it burns from the out-side-in, and therefore loses very little load-bearing strength as it burns.

The ability to own a home is central to the American Dream. Sadly, this is no longer an option for so many Americans. Not only are houses more expensive than they have ever been, but they are also located on smaller plots of land, and are no longer built to last.

As we have seen, the same is true of just about everything Americans buy—the appliances we rely on and the food we eat have be swapped out from under our noses. These processes have harmed America's families, and as we shall see in the next chapter, have endangered America itself.

CHAPTER 3

TWILIGHT OF THE GODS; ON AMERICA'S INDUSTRIAL DECLINE

B aldur, son of Odin and Frigg, was the most beloved of the Norse gods. It was prophesized that his death would bring about *Ragnarök*—the end of the world. In order to protect Baldur, his mother forced every entity in the cosmos to swear an oath that they would do no harm to her beloved son. Everything but mistletoe swore this oath.

One day the gods were playing a game—throwing deadly things at the invincible god Baldur and watching them bounce off him. Loki, jealous of Baldur's fame and glory, discovered that mistletoe could still harm Baldur. He tricked the blind god Hodur into throwing a spear made of mistletoe at Baldur, who died from the grievous wound. This unleashed the chain of events that brought about the end of Norse cosmology.

Baldur was the fulcrum upon which Norse Mythology turned. In the same way, America's economy tetters upon the health of our manufacturing sector.

And just as Baldur's death harkens the end of the Asgard, so too will the death of America's manufacturing sector bring about the economic collapse of our nation.

Consider that in World War II, America produced the gauze, iodine, and syringes that allowed allied troops to soldier on in the face of bloodshed and broken bones. Times have changed. Covid-19 has made it abundantly clear that America can no longer make basic medical supplies. For example, at the start of the government's pandemic response, Alexa Azar, President Donald Trump's Human Services secretary, noted that the President's response would require 25 times as many masks as had been stockpiled, and that it would take years for domestic manufacturers to fulfill the orders placed by America's Strategic National Stockpile.

Masks were just the tip of the iceberg. As it turns out, America's entire manufacturing base has been hollowed-out over the last 50 years. In this chapter we will survey the damage. I will show you the former glory of America's industrial age, and then the rapid decline. Specifically, we will look at how many manufacturing jobs have been lost, how this has impacted our ability to manufacture basic products, and how America's industrial decline has destroyed many of America's cities.

A SACRIFICE OF HIMSELF, UNTO HIMSELF

The United States was one of the first nations in the world to industrialize. In fact, the American Revolution was in no small part a product of the economic rivalry between the Thirteen Colonies and Great Britain.

From the founding of Jamestown in 1607 until the first shots were fired at Lexington in 1775, the economic relationship between Britain and her American colonies was *mercantile* in nature. Mercantilism ensured that the Colonies bought manufactured goods, like firearms and fabric, from Britain, in exchange for raw materials, like furs and tobacco. This resulted in the Colonies running a trade deficit with Britain.

Mercantilism was a boon for British industry, which benefited from increased demand for their products. Consider that by the 1770s nearly one-in-five British men worked in manufacturing. This high employment was buoyed by colonial demand for British products. In fact, demand from Colonies alone accounted for 72% of the growth in British manufacturing between 1700 and 1773.[25] During this period, the percentage of manufactured goods as an overall proportion of British exports grew from 4% to 27.4%. Likewise, Britain's trade surplus with the Colonies grew from £67,000 (1721-30) to £739,000 (1761-70)—in a few decades it was eleven times as big.[26] Essentially, British industry was piggybacking on American markets.

While Britain reaped the rewards of mercantilism, the Colonies economies were hampered by the need to buy British goods. Businessmen sought to capitalize on this fact by investing in domestic factories. Eventually, Britain cracked-down on these ventures. For example, in the 1750s Britain banned the construction of new iron-slitting mills in the Colonies,[27] and in 1775 Britain outlawed the production of steel products and certain industrial equipment.[28]

Britain even went so far as to ban the export of cloth-making technology to the Colonies. They did this by criminalizing the export of blueprints or machinery, and even prohibited industry specialists from going abroad. [29] These overbearing, and transparent attempts to lock the Colonies into economic subservience to Britain, were an important—but rarely discussed—catalyst for the American Revolution.

The *Declaration of Independence* was signed on July 4, 1776, and from there the rest is history—but it almost was not. The Revolution went badly at first. Not only did the Continental Army have little training or experience, but the Colonies lacked industrial production. Simply put, the Colonies were unable to produce enough gunpowder, firearms, knives, or uniforms for their armies. it was not until other European powers—in particular, France—supplied the Colonies with weapons that the tide of the war began to turn.[30]

After Cornwallis' surrender at Yorktown in 1781, and the subsequent *Treaty of Paris* in 1783, America was free—but only on paper. In practice, America still relied heavily on European imports to maintain her economy, military, and her independence. Freedom is a sham if it cannot be defended. No firearms, no freedom.

To remedy this situation, George Washington signed the *Tariff Act* of 1789.[31] In addition to raising much-needed tax revenue, the Act's purpose was to make British manufacturing more expensive, and to encourage the Americans to buy Made-in-America products. The *American System*—and American School economics—was born.

Despite the Founding Father's efforts—George Washington and Alexander Hamilton deserve special credit—industrialization was a slow process. Things changed after the War of 1812, when Britain's naval blockade emphasized just how dependent upon imports America remained.

Congress took action and passed the *Tariff Act* of 1816. This unified America's tariff policy, which was at that point a patchwork quilt of different tax rates imposed on different products. It also doubled the average tariff rates.[32] Relatively high tariffs remained the norm in America until the 1970s.

Interestingly—and this fact is largely buried by the mainstream media—most of America's greatest presidents supported tariffs, not free trade. Consider the following quotes:

> *...not only the wealth; but the independence and security of a Country, [is] materially connected with the prosperity of manufactures. Every nation, with a view to those great objects, ought to endeavour to possess within itself all the essentials of national supply.*

> ~Alexander Hamilton[33]

> *A free people ought not only to be armed, but disciplined; to which end a uniform and well-digested plan is requisite; and their safety and*

interest require that they should promote such manufactories as tend to render them independent of others for essential, particularly military, supplies...

~George Washington[34]

...experience has taught me that manufactures are now as necessary to our independence as to our comfort: and if those who quote me as of a different opinion will keep pace with me in purchasing nothing foreign where an equivalent of domestic fabric can be obtained, without regard to difference of price...

~Thomas Jefferson[35]

Give us a protective tariff and you will some day see the greatest nation the sun ever shone over. [36]

I do not know much... but I know this... when we buy manufactured goods abroad, we get the goods and the foreigner gets the money. When we buy the manufactured goods at home, we get both the goods and the money. [37]

~Abraham Lincoln

For centuries England has relied on protection, has carried it to extremes and has obtained satisfactory results from it. There is no doubt that it is to this system that it owes its present strength.

~Ulysses S. Grant[38]

The country has acquiesced in the wisdom of the protective-tariff principle. It is exceedingly undesirable that this system should be destroyed or that there should be violent and radical changes therein. Our past experience shows that great prosperity in this country has always come under a protective tariff.

~Theodore Roosevelt[39]

It was under the American System of tariffs—which were supported by every president featured on Mount Rushmore—that the United States transformed from an agricultural backwater into an industrial juggernaut.

By 1870 America was the second largest industrial power in the world, behind only Great Britain. In fact, 23% of all global industrial production was made in the United States.[40] America surpassed Britain in the 1880s, and remained the largest industrial powerhouse until 2010, when we were overtaken by China. At this point, America's share of global industrial output has fallen down to 16.8%—less than half of America's peak global production, and just over half of China's current industrial production.[41]

THE STING OF MISTLETOE

In 1979 just over 19,500,000 Americans worked in manufacturing jobs. These jobs paid well, had reasonable working hours, and often came with benefits like a pension or health insurance. By 2019—before the government's Covid response put the economy on ice—the number of Americans with manufacturing jobs declined to 11,700,000.

This means that in the last forty years America has lost just some 7,800,000 manufacturing jobs. Not coincidentally, most of these jobs were lost after 2001, when China jointed the World Trade Organization.

In Chapter 5 we will explore how unfair trade with China has been the driving force behind this job loss. But in the meantime, we will turn our attention to figuring out what happened to all of these people who lost their jobs, and what ripple effects that has had on America's economy.

First—and at this point it should go without saying—many Americans who lost their jobs have since been either permanently or chronically unemployed. As we saw in Chapter 1, the unemployment rate is far larger than the government's official number, and the rate has been increasing ever since the 1980s. This corresponds to the time that America's factories began closing down and moving abroad. No surprises there.

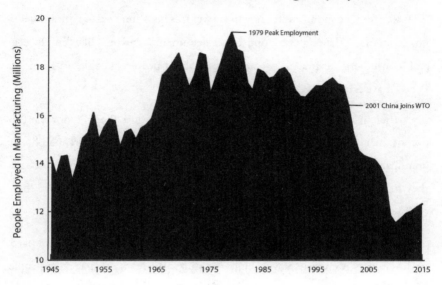

American Manufacturing Employment

The next question is why so many people—millions in fact—would stop working altogether. After all, people still need to eat, and food costs money. There are three main answers to this question. The first answer boils down to geography.

American industry was highly concentrated along America's northeast Atlantic coast and the Great Lakes region. Not only that, but many of the towns in this region were built to house and provide services for the factory workers. People worked at the local factory their whole lives and retired in the communities that they had built. They spent their money on electricians to wire their houses, hairdressers for their wives, and teachers for their children.

Ultimately, these factory towns—including all of the lawyers, bankers, and tradesmen who lived in town—depended upon the factory workers to support the local economy. When the factories closed down, the local economies slowly ground to a halt. As a result, many stopped working because there was no more work available. Essentially: no factory, no town; no town, no jobs.

This raises an obvious question: why not move somewhere else for work? "Conservative" economists struggle to answer this question because the answer is not economic. Although economists use dehumanizing words like "employees" and "consumers", ultimately, we are talking about people. People have homes. People have families. People have communities.

There is little doubt that many people stayed because they did not want to uproot their children from the family home. Perhaps they had elderly parents or grandparents who could not move, and they stayed to care for them. Or perhaps they loved their neighborhood or their church and did not want to leave their entire social lives behind.

We need to remember that the idea that people can move to different parts of the country is entirely new in human history. The reality is that most people have stayed where they were, and have done so not just for generations, but for millennia. For example, recent DNA analysis shows that Italian Americans are typically able to trace their ancestry back to specific villages in Italy, where people have been genetically isolated for well over a thousand years. Most people die where they were born. A factory closure is not likely to change this fundamental human trait.

The second reason that so many factory workers remained unemployed is because of human biology. We need to remember that although the human brain is plastic—that is it can grow and rewire itself in response to novel stimuli—this plasticity diminishes with age. As a result, it can be very difficult for someone who has worked the same job for ten, twenty, or thirty years, to re-train to do something entirely different. Unfortunately, there is truth in the folk expression "you cannot teach an old dog new tricks".

People are also limited by their individual levels of intelligence, aptitudes, temperament, and talents. It is simply not always possible for a factory worker to "learn to code", as the media constantly suggests; nor is it fair to say that a factory worker who enjoys working with his hands *want* to learn to code anyways. Because of these human limitations, many former factory workers remained unemployed because they could not work other jobs, even if they were available.

The third reason that many Americans have remained chronically unemployed has to do with the ways in which people chose to cope with the destruction of their communities. Many people—millions in fact—turned to drugs. In many cases we are talking about people who were initially prescribed medication by their family doctor to treat their depression or chronic pain. Many unemployed Americans became dependent, and eventually addicted to these prescription drugs. And so, the opioid epidemic was born.

In 2019 more than 70,000 Americans died from drug overdoses, and some 70% of these deaths were caused by opioids.[42] Many on the right blame these individuals for their choices. Those on the left blame the pharmaceutical industry.

Reality is not this clear cut. Yes, people make choices, and yes, the pharmaceutical industry is predatory by nature, however, most of the people who have been impacted by the opioid epidemic were not part of America's criminal underbelly—they were hardworking and proud blue collar white Americans whose lives unravelled, whose communities fell apart, and there was nothing that they could do to stop it.

As we shall see, the cause for this destruction rests firmly in Washington's hands, and we should not be quick to judge our brothers and sisters who are down on their luck for the machinations of bureaucrats hundreds of miles away.

Tying into this is how the government handled the factory closures. When faced with the looming crisis of job loss the government sprang into action. Did they attempt to shore-up America's industrial base? No. Instead, they cut cheques to the unemployed. Those who were chronically unemployed often applied for and received welfare cheques for illnesses or injuries that they had previously ignored or worked with.

As we saw in Chapter 1, the number of Americans claiming disability income from Social Security increased by some 13.6% between 2004 and 2014. Unfortunately, direct welfare payments have prolonged the period of recovery by allowing many people to survive in an economic climate otherwise devoid of hope. People can become addicted to welfare just as they become addicted to drugs. The government feeds this addiction, and in doing so makes a bad problem worse.

To summarize: America has lost almost 8 million manufacturing jobs since 1979. During the same period, the average unemployment rate was roughly 50% higher than it was during the postwar years—and the number itself is at least twice what the government claims anyways. As it stands there are well over 12 million unemployed Americans, and another 8 million working part-time jobs when they would rather work full time.

Factory closures have caused job loss, and much of this job loss is chronic due to the fact that it was geographically concentrated, human biology prevented many people from retraining. To make matters worse, our collective response to deindustrialization hamstrings our ability to address the real issues.

The chronic mass unemployment caused by America's factory closures has had other ripple effects. Chiefly, wages have stagnated or declined, depending on where you are. For example, factory workers who were lucky enough to find new jobs took an average pay cut of 17.5%.[43] This is a large amount of money—the difference between earning $50,000 and $40,000 per year. And this was just the immediate effect. In the long run, the flood of displaced workers drove wages down and decoupled American worker's wages from their productivity.

Consider that between 1950 and 1973, workers were paid according to their productivity. If they made more, they earned more. This justified annual raises which were both fair and sustainable in the long run. However, this paradigm changed. Worker productivity has increased by 72% since 1973, and yet their real wages have not increased.[44]

Growth in productivity and hourly compensation since 1948

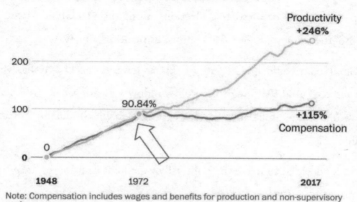

Note: Compensation includes wages and benefits for production and non-supervisory workers

Source: Economic Policy Institute

What this means in practical terms is that Americans are producing more wealth than ever before, and yet they are increasingly unable to afford to buy the fruits of their labor. This is the exact opposite of what America's foremost historical industrialists—like Henry Ford—wanted. Henry Ford was a big proponent of paying workers enough to buy what they produced. In doing so, he not only built automobiles, but he also built a market for automobiles. We lost this wisdom somewhere along the way.

THE SLAYING OF FAFNIR

There is a reason that 1973 was such an inflection point in the U.S. economy. On August 15, 1971 President Richard Nixon had announced the closing of the gold window, which came to be known as the "Nixon Shock." Thanks to the

Nixon White House tapes, we now know *why* Nixon made this fateful decision which set the United States on a path to financial ruin.

On 26 July 1971, Nixon was recorded saying, "I've never seen anybody beaten on inflation in the United States. I've seen many people beaten on unemployment." Unemployment had increased from 3.4% when he took office to over 6% by 1971. He took the drastic action he did with an eye on cutting the unemployment rate before the 72 election, urging the Fed Chair Arthur Burns to "goose" the money supply. Also known as printing money.

But Nixon could not do any of this as long as the U.S. dollar was tied to the price of gold. Although the gold window was not a true gold standard, it prevented trade imbalances and was a reasonable brake on government spending.

So he decided to make the politically expedient decision to drop the gold window with the stroke of a pen.

As might have been predicted, the move had disastrous consequences. Indeed, Fed Chairman Burns warned at the time that the U.S. balance of payments would go from a surplus to a deficit.

The fact is that the chronic trade deficits we face today would never have been possible under a gold standard, for the simple reason that a gold standard dictates that trade deficits must be balanced by paying the trade surplus country in gold to compensate it for the exchange of goods. The consequence of Nixon's new easy money policy was that henceforth trade deficits never had to be balanced.

The other entirely predictable consequence was inflation. Now that the government could print money at will, there was no longer a restraint on the growth of the money supply. Inflation is a direct result of an increase in the money supply.

There is no better example of the devastating result of money printing than the enduring effects of the COVID-19 "economic relief" spending bill. Using 2019 as a benchmark:

	2019	2023	Percentage Change
Value of $10 (official gov't inflation rate)	$10	$8.16	-18.4%
Value of $10 (Shadow-Stats inflation rate)	$10	$6.15	-38.5%
M2 Money Supply	$14.8 trillion	$20.8 trillion	40.5%
Average Price of Home	$382,700	$521,900[1]	36%
Average Rent Per Month	$1,149	$1,448[2]	26%
Average Wage	$27.90	$33.91[3]	21.5%

The Bureau of Labor Statistics (BLS) changed the composition and weight of the basket of goods used to calculate the consumer price index in both the 1980s and the 1990s. ShadowStats calculates its inflation rate based off the BLS formula from the 1980s. Does it feel to you that you have only lost 18% of your purchasing power or 38% since 2019?

The decoupling of worker productivity and compensation, wage increases trailing the inflation rate, the rise in income inequality, our chronic trade deficits and government deficits etc. can all be traced to the closing of the gold window. Because without any sort of mechanism of restraint, politicians will always choose the easy road. And the easy road is to keep the printing presses going.

TO FORGE GULLINBURSTI

Our politicians claim that they are not to blame for Americans losing their manufacturing jobs—it has nothing to do with NAFTA or our trade deficit with China. Instead, they blame automation. Robots, not Mexicans, are taking our jobs! This could not be further from the truth.

In 1908 Henry Ford, one of America's greatest industrialists, released his latest and greatest automobile, the Model T. What made the Model T so special was its price tag: the Model T cost just $850, which works out to approximately $21,000 in 2019 currency. This was a watershed moment in American history. For the first time ever, the automobile was accessible to more than the handful of wealthy hobbyists who had until then been the only ones who could afford them. Ford spent the next few years exploring ways to cut costs, so that he could realize his dream of bringing automobiles to the masses.

In December of 1913, the Ford Motor Company opened the world's first factory with a mobile assembly line. This factory was an order of magnitude more efficient than any of its predecessors, and Ford was able to reduce the time it took to build a Model T from 12 hours to just 93 minutes.[45]

Greater efficiency led to greater production. In 1914 Ford produced 308,162 Model Ts—more automobiles than all other manufacturers combined. It also led to lower prices. By 1924 a new Model T cost just $260, or roughly $3,500 in 2019 currency. This was fully 83 percent cheaper than what a Model T cost just a decade early. The Automobile Age had begun.

The moral of this story is that Henry Ford's automations greatly reduced the need for human labor, making most of his workers redundant. And yet, Henry Ford did not fire his workers. He hired many more. In fact, the number of Americans working in factories continued to increase until 1979, half a century *after* Henry Ford made his workers redundant. How is this possible?

At a bare-bones level, employment is determined by the ratio between *productivity* and *output*. All other things being equal: higher productivity, getting more done each hour, means fewer jobs, while higher output, making more stuff, means more jobs. If both productivity and output increase at the same rate, then employment is not affected.

Imagine, for example, an all-American car company called Aspen Automobiles. Aspen makes 1,000 vehicles every year at its factory, which employs 100 workers. In 2016 the automaker got lucky, selling out of its popular Poplar Crossover. Given the company's success, Aspen has big plans for 2017, with 100 extra Poplar Crossovers expected to roll off the assembly line. This means Aspen must hire 10 more workers, since 10 percent more output requires 10 percent more labor. This is how increasing output—also known as economic growth—creates jobs.

Now let us add another factor into the equation. Pretend 2016 was a normal year, and Aspen does not think it could sell more vehicles in 2017. Nevertheless, Aspen is determined to make more money. Therefore, the company invests in a few robotic welding torches that allow line workers to weld much faster than they did before.

This improves the factory's efficiency by 10 percent. Now Aspen can make the same number of vehicles with only 90 employees. In this case, higher productivity via automation cost workers their jobs.

Now combine the two factors: 2016 was a great year, and Aspen decides to go ahead and make 100 extra vehicles. Not only that, but the company also invests in the robotic welding torches, making the factory 10 percent more efficient. What happens to the workers?

On the one hand, Aspen needs more employees to make more vehicles; on the other, the manufacturer needs fewer workers because of automation. Overall, employment is not affected in a meaningful way because the two factors cancel each other out: Aspen could make more vehicles with the same number of employees. This is what makes an economy more prosperous. The takeaway: if productivity and output increase or decrease at the same rate, employment does not change.

Now, let us apply the above logic to America's manufacturing industry. Between 1950 and 1979, manufacturing employment increased because output grew faster than productivity. This changed over the next decade. By the 1990s, the historic balance was upset. Between 1989 and 2000 American manufacturing output grew by 3.7 percent on average, while productivity grew by 4.1 percent—employment consequently declined.

Since 2000, output growth nosedived: output grew only 0.4 percent per year, on average, while productivity increased at a rate of 3.7 percent. As a result, America shed more than 4 million manufacturing jobs. Clearly automation is not to blame for America's manufacturing job loss. The real culprit is America's trade deficit, which we will explore in Chapter 5.

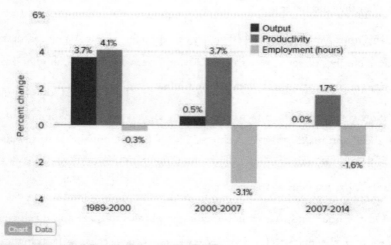

Average annual change in output, productivity, and employment growth in U.S. manufacturing, 1989–2014

Source: EPI analysis of Bureau of Labor Statistics (2015b)

Economic Policy Institute

IF YMIR WERE HOLLOW

America has lost more than jobs: we lost our ability to make the things that we use every day. For example, America no longer mass-produces items as basic as dress shirts, spoons, or forks. [46] If those items seem trivial to you, consider that America no longer builds laptops—save for one, ironically Chinese-owned factory—smartphones, or televisions. [47]

Even at a more fundamental level, America does not even have the ability to manufacture sufficient numbers of semiconductors, which are used to create just about every modern electronic device, from lamps to cars to supercomputers. In fact, America does not even manufacture—nor does it have the ability to manufacture—the photolithography equipment required to build modern semiconductors. Those machines are built in the Netherlands, while the semiconductors themselves are build primarily in Asia.

This is a massive problem. It is not an understatement to suggest that America cannot properly function without access to laptops and smartphones, and yet we are almost entirely reliant upon foreign nations, mainly China, to sustain our material wellbeing. We received a taste of this danger during Covid, when shortages in new vehicles occurred because of supply chain issues with Chinese motherboards. This problem will only grow in urgency.

Although this is concerning, what is even more concerning is the fact that America no longer manufactures enough of the sorts of basic machinery that is required to manufacture simple household items—never mind the sophisticated electrical components needed for computers and smartphones. In other words, even if we wanted to manufacture forks, we would probably need to buy the fork-making machinery from China.

This is made clear when we look at America's production of *machine tools*. A machine tool is a piece of machinery that shapes its output by removing material by way of lathing, planning, drilling, milling, grinding, sawing, or pressing the output. Machine tools transform raw materials into something useful. They are the tools that make tools.

America used to be the leading manufacturer and global exporter of machine tools. Today, America imports of most its machine tools, and only produces 7% of the world's machine tools. For comparison, Italy produces 8%, while China makes 29%.[48]

Machine tool producers' market share in 2020, by country

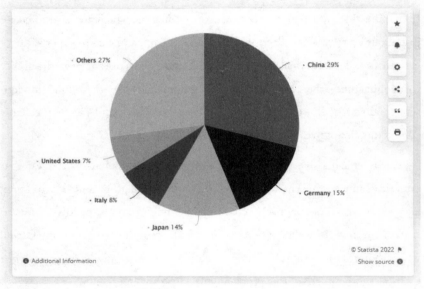

Many "conservative" politicians spin America's inability to produce forks and knives as a good sign: why should we waste our time building cutlery when we could be building aircraft? American industry is not being hollowed out; it is moving up the value chain. This argument, however, does not hold any water.

The truth is that even America's most *advanced industries*—aeronautics, information technologies, and pharmaceuticals—are moving abroad. A report by the Brookings Institute explored this in some detail. The begin with, they define advanced industries as those which satisfied two metrics.

First, the industry as a whole must spend more in research and development than 80% of other American industries. Second, over 21% of the industry's workforce must have advanced training or education in the STEM fields.[49] These advanced industries are very important because they produce over $3 trillion worth of output, employ 80% of America's engineers, file 85% of patents, and provide 90% of private sector research and development funding.

Not only that, but our advanced industries are America's primary *anchor industries*. They create new wealth, much like the factories did in the Rustbelt or gold mines did in the Yukon. They also support large supply chains. Estimates suggest that some 27.1 million jobs ultimately depend upon the health of America's advanced industries. In short, advanced industries are very important for America's economy, and they too are rotting away.

For example, in 1980, 59 of America's 100 largest cities were "innovation capitals", meaning more than 10% of their labor force worked in advanced industries. By 2013, only 23 could still be classified as innovation capitals.[50]

This is hurting America's inventive spirit: when looking at the number of global patent cooperation treaty applications per capita, which is a rough estimate for the number of significant inventions made per person, we find that only 2 American cities—San Diego and San Jose—break the top 20 globally.[51] Americans used to dominate this category, not anymore. Other countries are picking up the slack.

Not only has America's share of global research fallen faster than our share of the world's GDP, meaning we are researching proportionally less, America has moved 38% of its research jobs abroad.[52] We are literally importing science. We are buying the future we should be building.

This is happening because America is importing ever-more advanced products. In 2019 alone America imported $495,478,000,000 worth of advanced technology products from abroad. This has helped to balloon America's trade deficit. In fact, some 56% of the increase in America's trade deficit in the last two decades has been in advanced goods. Basically, we are buying more of our most advanced technology, rather than inventing and building it at home.

This is made clear in the below graphs, taken from the OEC.[53] which show the growth in technological sophistication of America's exports from China between 2001 and 2021. I have also included the same graph, but this time for exports. As you can see, the exports show precisely the opposite. America is buying more technology, and exporting more raw materials. We are, in no uncertain terms, on the road to becoming China's mercantile resource colony.

United States Imports from China (2001)

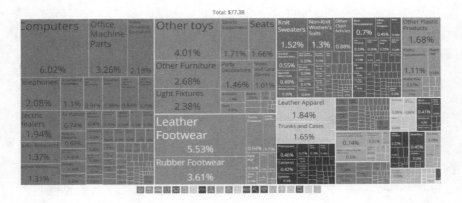

United States Imports from China (2021)

United States Exports to China (2001)

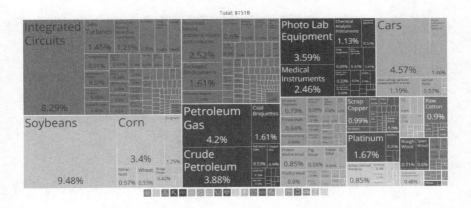

United States Exports to China (2021)

To be clear, this process is not occurring because foreigners make better stuff—nor do they make it more efficiently. America's advanced industries are the second most productive in the world, behind only Norway. Further, our industries were 50-70% more efficient than our Western competitors like Sweden, Italy, or Germany. Yet American industry is eroding, not Sweden's. Not Italy's. Not Germany's.[54]

America is currently in the process of deindustrialising—the mistletoe spear has already pierced our side. Just as Baldur's death set in motion the events of Ragnarök, so too has our manufacturing decline impoverished the American people and weakened the American nation. Unless we can reverse the trend, America will continue to slide into oblivion, only to be devoured by our economic rivals.

PART II

PRAISING CATO: HOW THE TRADE DEFICIT DESTROYED AMERICA

Two thousand years ago the West was dominated by two rival cities: Rome and Carthage. Each was set to overpower the others at various times. Rome was at the brink of defeat during the Second Punic War, when Hannibal of Carthage led his army—resplendent with its gaudy train of African war elephants—through the Alps and into Italy.

Hannibal fought the Romans on their turf, slaughtering hundreds of thousands of young men in their prime. The bloodshed continued for decades, until the brilliant Scipio Africanus forced Hannibal to return to Africa to defend his homeland. Scipio defeated Hannibal at the Battle of Zama (202 BC).

The enmity between Rome and Carthage could not assuaged with promises of friendship or gifts of gold. In the following decades Senator Cato the Censor ceaselessly called for Carthage's extermination. He infamously ended every speech—no matter the topic—with the phrase *Carthago delenda est*: "and furthermore, Carthage must be destroyed".

Cato's persistence paid off. Rome sacked Carthage in the Third Punic War. Rome sold the Carthaginians into slavery and sowed their fields with salt. Carthage never rose again.

Although Cato's strategy may seem juvenile—like a child asking for a new toy day and night—it was profoundly effective. Repetition works.

This is because the human brain is hardwired to think subconsciously using mental shortcuts. These shortcuts are called *heuristics*. These heuristics lead to certain biases and blind spots in our cognition and perception. Once such a thought has been formed by the subconscious, it can be very hard to shake. It rattles around in the mind like a pebble in the shoe until it is acknowledged.

By repeating the phrase *Carthago delenda est* day in and day out, Cato engaged directly with his audiences' subconscious minds. He did this by conditioning his listeners to associate himself—and the senate itself—with destroying Carthage. Every time a senator saluted Cato or walked into the building itself, they could not help but think of Cato's words. They were psychologically *primed* to vote to destroy Carthage.

The human mind also uses heuristics to make snap judgements about whether something is probable. Essentially, the easier the brain can retrieve a piece of information, because it heard the information recently and frequently, the more likely the brain is to use it in forming your opinions and beliefs. This is called the *availability heuristic*.

To sum up, hearing about the destruction of Carthage every day made Romans more likely to believe that Carthage would be destroyed—that Carthage *must* be destroyed.

Today's propagandists do exactly what Cato did over two millennia ago. They repeat the same talking points day and night—on television, on the radio, on the internet—until people start to believe them. After all, something so ubiquitous could not be that bad, or so the subconscious mind assumes. In this way, Americans have been conditioned to reflexively oppose tariffs. Instead, Americans support free trade, mostly because this is the only option presented in the public discourse.

In Part I of this book, we surveyed America's economic problems. In Part II we will see how the trade deficit is at the root of these economic problems, as well as a host of other social, political, and environmental problems that few are willing to discuss. Furthermore, America needs tariffs.

CHAPTER 4

DOCTOR FAUSTUS' TRAGICAL BARGAIN, OR HOW TRADE DEFICITS WORK

Had I as many souls as there be stars,

I'd give them all for Mephistophilis.

~ Doctor Faustus

Spectators claim that Satan himself appeared on stage during the opening performance of Christopher Marlowe's play *Doctor Faustus* (1588)—the grizzly specter drove men mad with fear. Some wanted to demolish the theater, others to hang Marlowe for his occult summoning. In spite of this controversy, or perhaps because of it, the play was a hit. Today *Faustus* remains one of the greatest works of literature. Why?

Exquisite language?—lines like "the face that launch'd a thousand ships" have haunted readers for centuries. Perhaps. But time rarely preserves art for art's sake: what survives is *useful*, it serves a purpose. *Doctor Faustus* is no exception.

The plot is simple: Faustus sells his soul to Satan in exchange for the demon Mephisophilis' service for twenty-four years. Faustus dreams of wealth: I will "wall all Germany with brass...fill the public schools with silk" and "live a life of all voluptuousness." In the end, Faustus wastes his power and Satan takes his soul. The tragedy of Doctor Faustus contains an important lesson worth heeding: never trade tomorrow for today.

Unfortunately, that is exactly what America is doing. America has run a trade deficit every year for the last forty years. In 2019 the American trade deficit in goods topped $845 billion. How do we pay for deficits? Rather than selling our own current output, things that we make, we sell our past output, assets, and the promise of future production, debt. And why is America selling her very soul? Because, like Doctor Faustus, our appetite for imported "voluptuousness" exceeds are rational expectations, and our love of today overshadows our fear of tomorrow.

America *is* Faustus—and we are running out of soul to sell.

FOR LOVE OF THEE, I CUT MINE ARM...

We will begin by answering the most basic question: what is a *trade deficit?* Simply put, a trade deficit occurs when one country imports (buys) more than it exports (sells) to another country during a specific time period. Usually, we look at the numbers over a yearly basis, because different countries buy and sell different things depending on the seasons.

For example, if America bought $100 worth of oranges from Japan in November, but only sold Japan $50 worth of apples in July, we could say that America ran a trade deficit of $50 with Japan during the year. Conversely, we could say that Japan ran a $50 *trade surplus* with America. The overall difference, whether a surplus or a deficit, is known as the *balance of trade.*

Of course, in real life America buys more than oranges and sells more than apples. We buy and sell all kinds of *goods*, that is, physical products from apples to iPhones to cars. Therefore, when media personalities talk about the trade deficit, they usually refer to the overall trade deficit in goods—the deficit between all physical products bought and sold by America from all other countries in a given year.

In 2019, America's trade deficit was $845,759,200,000. That is, we bought over $845 *billion* more goods than we sold in 2019. This works out to $5,443 for every working American. To put this into perspective, this is roughly equivalent to having imported the entire annual GDP of a country like Indonesia, Turkey, or the Netherlands.

Not only is America's trade deficit objectively large, but America has run a trade deficit in goods every year since 1974—and this trade deficit grows almost every year. The cumulative effects of this chronic trade deficit cannot be overstated. Consider that since 2001, when China joined the World Trade Organization, America has racked-up a cumulative trade deficit of $13.2 *trillion*. This works out to some $84,019 for every working American citizen. This number grows continues to grow.

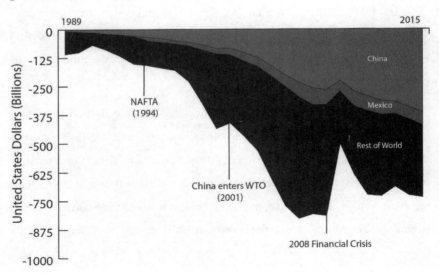

America runs a large, chronic trade deficit. However, this does not mean that we run a trade deficit with every country. A closer inspection of the numbers reveals that America generally has a balanced trade relationship with economically developed countries. Meanwhile, America typically runs trade deficits with developing countries.

SI PECCASSE NEGAMUS, FALLIMUR, ET NULLA EST IN NOBIS VERITAS

The next logical question is how does America pay for the trade deficit? There are four—and only four—ways for a country to acquire foreign goods. First, they could obtain them by way of tribute, either through of gifts or coercion. Second, they could obtain them by *trading* goods for goods. Third, they can do so by *selling* assets. Fourth, they can obtain goods by *promising* to pay in the future. Although each of these options have been historically important, America's current predicament places us squarely within options three and four. Let us explore each of the ways for countries to obtain foreign goods in more detail.

The first way that a country may obtain foreign goods is through *tribute*. Tribute simply refers to products received by one country from another country without a reciprocal exchange of products, either now or in the future. Essentially, tribute is a free lunch.

Although tribute is fairly rare today, it has historically been the most common way that countries have enriched themselves, and it explains most of the vast differences in wealth between historical societies. Tribute may take the form of gifts given from one country to another for the purposes of strengthening relationships. For example, the United States received the Statue of Liberty from France as tribute, due to the two countries' historical friendship.

More commonly, tribute takes the form of coercion wherein one country provides products to another because of an asymmetrical political relationship. Often, weak countries would pay tribute to strong countries to prevent an invasion, and just as frequently weak countries would be looted by strong countries. In both cases the transfer of products can be characterized as tribute.

Tribute was exceedingly common in history. For example, client states of the Persian Empire were required to provide tribute to the Great King as diverse as horses from Cilicia, eunuchs from Assyria, or gold from India. Likewise, the Spanish Empire obtained fabulous quantities of gold, silver, and exotic plants and animals from their conquest of the Aztec and Inca civilizations.

Although the prospect of obtaining products by way of tribute is fascinating, it is irrelevant for our discussion of America's trade deficit. China is not giving us our semiconductors because they like us, nor has America invaded Guatemala for the purposes of securing an unlimited supply of bananas—at least not recently.

The second way that countries can acquire foreign goods is by trading. That is, countries may exchange currently-produced output for currently-produced output. For example, Argentina sells steaks to America in exchange for automobiles. If the value of steaks and automobiles is equal, then trade is balanced, and no further payment is required.

Of course, a country's output is not limited to goods, and therefore our discussion of the trade deficit has until this point been somewhat misleading. America exports both goods and *services*. As we have discussed, a *good* is a physical commodity—something that you can touch, taste, or smell, like a brick, an apple, or a bottle of perfume. Goods can be owned, stored, and consumed by the buyer after they are produced.

A *service*, on the other hand, is not a physical product that can be owned, stored, or consumed later. Instead, a service is something that is intangible which is usually produced and consumed simultaneously. Typically, services deal in convenience and information. A helpful example that highlights the distinction between goods and services can be found in the music industry.

Our grandparents used to buy music on vinyl records. The vinyl record was a good which they bought: it was a physical product which transferred ownership from the seller to the buyer, and could be stored on the shelf until someone wanted to listen. Presently, many people listen to music on Spotify: they sign into their account and stream music from the application. Spotify does not sell any physical products, the listener does not own anything new, and the music cannot be stored because it is only available so long as the listener has a Spotify account. Spotify is a classic example of a service. Other examples include massages, legal representation in court, or business consulting.

Selling services is tremendously lucrative—services underpin the entire business model of Silicon Valley—and they form a large portion of America's exports. In fact, America had a trade surplus in services worth $288.9 billion in 2019. This means that a portion of America's trade deficit in goods was offset by America's trade surplus in services.

Overall, America's goods *and* services trade deficit is worth $557 billion—this remains an enormous amount. Given that America runs a deficit in total current output, our initial question remains unanswered: how does America pay for the trade deficit?

HOMO FUGE: YET SHALL NOT FAUSTUS FLY

The third way that countries acquire foreign products is by *selling* past output, something that was made in the past but retains value today. That is, the country must sell its *assets*. A good example of an asset is a house. The production of a house made in 1973 would contribute towards America's GDP in 1973, but not today.

However, the house—or perhaps more accurately, the land upon which it is built—retains value and can be sold in the current year to buy foreign products. This sale would not count towards America's GDP, nor would it factor into the trade deficit, however, it is an integral component of the *balance of payments*.

When discussing international trade, many economists contend that trade deficits do not exist because they are only one half of the balance of payments—they are simply a part of a larger equation. For example, Professor Steve Hanke of Johns Hopkins University writes that "the U.S. trade deficit… is just the mirror image of what is happening in the U.S. domestic economy. If expenditures in the U.S. exceed the incomes produced in the U.S., which they do, the excess expenditures will be met by an excess of imports over exports (read: a trade deficit)."[55]

What Hanke and other liberal economists fail to recognize are the practical consequences of running a trade deficit. Although the books are balanced on paper, reality shows us that it matters *how* they are balanced—there are two sides to every coin, but heads is not tails.

Every year, America sells billions worth of assets to pay for the trade deficit. To be clear, selling assets is not always a bad deal. For example, my law firm recently sold some old (ugly) furniture and used the proceeds to buy desktop scanners for our support staff. In this case we turned assets which did little more than take up space into assets that increase worker productivity. This was a good deal.

On the other hand, if I had sold my life-sized marble bust of Julius Caesar and used the proceeds to buy pizza, this would have been a bad deal. Not only would I lose out on any profits from the statue's appreciation, but I would have nothing to show of the proceeds after I ate the pizza. There is an important economic difference between fine art and pizza—between the permanent and the impermanent—between investing and consuming. *Context* matters, and this is a lesson which is lost on liberal economists.

Unfortunately, this lesson is also lost on America's leaders. America is selling hundreds of billions worth of assets—everything from shares in New York's largest companies to Iowa's best farmland—every year to pay for our trade deficit. For example, foreign investors now own some 40% of all U.S. equities. This has skyrocketed up from just 12% in 2007.[56]

Likewise, Americans are selling enormous amounts of real estate to pay for foreign production. In 2019 alone, foreigners purchased $183 billion in American real estate.[57] America is selling its heritage and its economic lifeblood for cheap Chinese trinkets. We are selling our soul for convenience.

The fourth, and final, way that countries can acquire foreign production is by *promising* to pay for it in the future. In other words, by buying it on credit with debt. This last option is how America funds the bulk of its trade deficit. Consider that foreigners now own 33% of America's national public debt, worth $7.7 *trillion.*[58] Likewise, America's household debt has climbed to unprecedented levels.

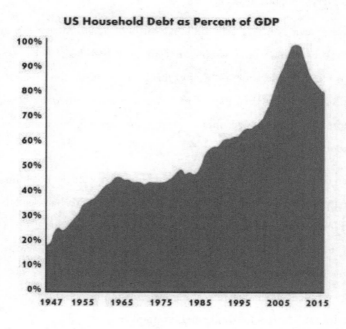

76

Debt is especially dangerous because not only does the borrower need to repay the principle, but will also need to repay the interest owed. This inflates the cost of buying foreign products in a way that most economists fail to appreciate. Consider that America became a *debtor nation* in 2006—for the first time since the Great Depression.[59]

This means that America paid more money in interest to foreign holders than it received from abroad. Currently, America pays $132 billion to foreigners each year in interest on our national public debt. This is about one quarter the value of our trade deficit, and it too is increasing every year.

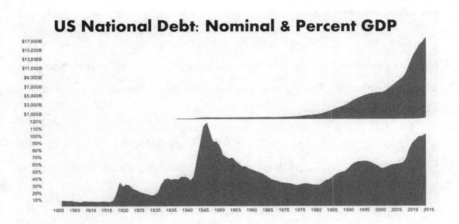

US National Debt: Nominal & Percent GDP

LENTE, LENTE CURRITE, NOCTIS EQUI!

In 2021 America's trade deficit topped $1 trillion. Although we pay for a portion of this deficit by trading services, we pay for the bulk of the trade deficit by selling assets and promising to pay with debt. Although this distinction is very clear in theory, in reality these components are often entangled. Nowhere is this more obvious, or damaging, than when it comes to corporate *offshore outsourcing*. Before explaining how this process works, we need to make sure that we are on the same page regarding the terminology.

Outsourcing occurs when an entity contracts with another entity to perform a specified process. For example, Faustus Industries owns a factory. The factory floors are dirty. They also have a janitor, but he is decrepit and overpaid. Therefore, Faustus Industries fires the janitor, and rather than hiring a new janitor, they hire Valdes Enterprises, a janitorial company, to clean the floors. In this case, Faustus outsourced its janitorial needs to Valdes. Outsourcing has pros and cons.

The major pro is that outsourcing allows for greater economic specialization, which can result in cost savings and higher quality work—a cleaning company will likely be more efficient at cleaning than a watchmaking company with a part-time janitor.

The major con is that the entity doing the outsourcing may lose control over the processes, and the contracted entity may not be as loyal as would an internal employee. Finally, it is important to note that outsourcing occurs within the domestic market.

Overall, outsourcing is good for the country because it helps to allocate labor and capital more efficiently within the country, which leads to more economic growth.

Offshoring occurs when an entity moves some of its operations abroad. Usually this is done by way of creating a foreign-based subsidiary company. For example, Faustus Industries builds cars in America. However, their executives learn that they can increase their profits by manufacturing the engines in Mexico. As a result, they incorporate Industrias Faustus, a wholly-owned subsidiary corporation, to build the engines in Mexico. In this case, Faustus Industries benefits from cheaper engines, and so do their customers.

Offshoring is a double-edged sword: in addition to the issues noted above respecting outsourcing, labor and capital are allocated more efficiently globally.

However, global efficiency does not necessarily mean that all entities will benefit from said efficiency.

Again, context matters. For example, pretend there is an American fast-food chain called McBurger. McBurger opens a restaurant in Shanghai. This unquestionably benefits McBurger, which reaps big profits from the new Chinese market. This restaurant likewise benefits America, because not only do American investors profit, but America as a whole loses no jobs, capital, or technical knowhow.

On the other hand, while offshoring can be profitable to individual entities, it can be very damaging to America as a whole. For example, assume that Faustus Industries has a research laboratory in Boston. Unfortunately, Bostonian scientists are both ornery and expensive. As a result, Faustus opens up a new research laboratory in Calcutta, India. Although this may benefit Faustus, it likely harms America by reducing the number of technologically sophisticated jobs in America, and the many spinoff benefits that these bring.

Finally, *offshore outsourcing* is a combination of the two terms: a domestic entity hires a foreign entity to perform a process in a foreign country. For example, if Faustus Industries hired Industrias Valdes to build its engines in Mexico, then it can be said to have offshore outsourced this part of its business. Although offshore outsourcing may be very lucrative to Faustus Industries, it is likely very damaging to America as a whole. For the sake of convenience, from this point on when I speak of *offshoring*, I am referring to *offshore outsourcing*.

O MERCY, HEAVEN! LOOK NOT SO FIERCE ON ME

When Doctor Faustus sacrificed his eternal soul for ephemeral delights, he cut his arm and swore a blood oath to Lucifer. Although this oath was not the cause of Faustus' tragedy—his hubris and his greed saw to that—the oath set in motion the chain of events which led to his damnation. Offshoring is America's blood oath. While it is not the cause of America's trade deficit, its perverse logic has made the trade deficit inevitable under current market conditions. This fact becomes obvious once you understand the offshoring *vicious cycle*.

Offshoring is not simply a sequence of events with a definitive start and end point. Instead, it is a repeating cycle, and much like a boulder rolling down a hill, it picks up speed with each rotation. The best way to understand how offshoring works is through a thought experiment. We will explore the raw data in Chapter 5.

To begin with, imagine that there are ten widget-making companies in America. Each company has one manager and nine factory workers. Each companies makes equally-good widgets, which they sell for $100 per widget. Eventually, one of the companies, Faustus Industries, discovers it can save money by making widgets in Japan and shipping them to America. Faustus Industries does just that, and sells its imported widgets for $80. Faustus also closes its redundant American factory and fires all 9 workers. It does, however, hire one new American manager to oversee its global operations. Faustus Industries clearly benefits from offshoring: cheaper widgets increase profits and help it undercut its competition. Overall, the impact on America's economy is negligible—nine people may have lost their jobs, but the remaining 91 workers benefit from cheaper widgets.

It does not take long for other companies to realize that Faustus Industries will outcompete them unless they too move their factories to Japan—after all, who would buy a widget for $100 when they can buy an equally-good widget for $80? The market has spoken. One by one the companies close their American factories until none remain. In the end, America is home to 90 unemployed factory workers and twenty rich managers. How do Americans continue to buy widgets? They sell their assets and promise to pay on their credit cards.

Of course, America does not just build widgets. We also build doohickeys. Assume that 100 Americans build doohickeys. Faustus Industries fires the first nine widget makers. What happens next? First, the widget makers apply for jobs building doohickies. Given the choice between unemployment and building doohickeys, these workers are willing to work for less than they used to—and perhaps more importantly, they are willing to work for less than their former coworkers.

Likewise, the doohickey managers are flooded with job applications, and realize that they can pay new hires less. They even use this as leverage to stop giving their old employees raises—they should be happy to even have jobs! The takeaway is that increased competition for doohickey-building jobs reduces wages in the doohickey industry.

The unemployed workers who could not find doohickey-building jobs eventually settled for jobs in the service industry. After all, Faustus Industries and the other widget companies hired more managers, and managers increase demand for services by spending money on restaurants and haircuts. Unfortunately, serving tables does not pay as much as making widgets. Likewise, managers only have so much hair to cut—they cannot support an unlimited number of service jobs.

At this point, offshoring has had three primary effects. First, it caused unemployment. All widget-makers lost their jobs in the short term, and some have been chronically unemployed ever since. Second, it reduced wages for workers in other industries. Doohickey builders now earn less because of increased competition for their jobs. The same is true of the service industry.

Third, offshoring increased inequality. This is because the factory workers were "replaced" with another manager. The manager earns more than the factory workers used to, and the factory workers now earn less. Although inequality is not in and of itself a bad thing, it can have destabilizing effects on the economy—and society more broadly—if left unchecked.

This is where the offshoring *vicious cycle* repeats. Because people earn less money, they start buying fewer widgets. Faustus Industries realizes that this is bad for business, and therefore moves their factory from Japan to Taiwan, which is even cheaper. They reduce the price of their widgets to $60.

The other companies follow their lead. However, reducing the price is just a short-term solution. Eventually, Americans are unable to afford $60 widgets. As such, Faustus Industries moves their factory to China, and drops prices even further. This cycle occurs until there is *nowhere* to make cheaper widgets. The promise of "cheap goods" given by offshoring is a fleeting sham. As it turns out, the race to the bottom has a finish line, and the checkered flag is Americans struggling to afford $1 widgets.

In the long run, the only way to permanently reduce prices is to increase productivity, that is, make more widgets in the same amount of time. Unfortunately, by moving factories to cheaper locations, Faustus Industries removed the most powerful economic incentive to invent and innovate—high labor costs. After all, why would you invest in labor-saving technology when labor is just about free? As we will see in Chapter 8, this process is how offshoring retards long-run economic growth.

The end result of the offshoring vicious cycle is the economic equivalent of Hieronymus Bosch's hellscape, the *Garden of Earthly Delights*. American workers earn less than their parent's generation, and struggle to afford even the "cheapest" widgets.

To make matters worse, America's rivals—like Japan and China—will build their own widgets rather than buying ours. And in a final ironic twist of fate, foreign widget manufacturers will eventually expand into the hollowed-out American widget market, since their foreign-designed-foreign-made, widgets are cheaper than our American-designed-foreign-made widgets.

Remember, the offshoring process is not limited to the widget making industry. Gizmos are also being offshored. So are doodads and whatchamacallits! *Anything* that can be done cheaper abroad may be subject to the offshoring vicious cycle. As it turns out, this includes most of America's most lucrative and strategically valuable industries—widgets being the first among equals, naturally.[iv]

When Doctor Faustus sacrificed his immortal soul for temporal delights, he did so not because he was stupid, but because he was smart. Faustus believed that he was exceptional. That he was brilliant. That he could surmise a way to evade his fate.

America's best and brightest have likewise deluded themselves into thinking that they can tame the offshoring vicious cycle. Our politicians ignore the problem, while our economists twist logic to justify our greed. However, like Faustus, America cannot obtain an infinite supply of imported voluptuousness for free. We must trade something, be it our past or our future, our sovereignty or our soul. Unless we change our course, we will be forced to accept our fate like the lamentable doctor:

Curs'd be the parents that engender'd me!

No, Faustus, curse thyself…

[for thou hast] depriv'd thee of the joys of heaven.

---

iv This is a fairly well-understood process which has been articulated by scholars much more distinguished than myself. I encourage you to explore this in more detail, here are some good places to start: *Outsourcing and Industrial Decline* by Richard A. Bettis, Stephen P. Bradley and Gary Hamel, & *Free Trade Doesn't Work: what should replace it and why*, Ian Fletcher, & *Three Billion New Capitalists: The Great Shift of Wealth and Power to the East* Clyde V. Prestowitz

CHAPTER 5

MORIARTY'S WEB, OR HOW THE TRADE DEFICIT DESTROYS AMERICA

There's a scarlet thread of murder running through the colourless skein of life, and our duty is to unravel it, and isolate it, and expose every inch of it.[60]

~ Sherlock Holmes

A *Study in Scarlet* was first published in the pages of the *Beeton's Christmas Annual* magazine in 1887. Although this marks the indomitable Sherlock Holmes' first appearance in the western literary canon, the novel attracted little immediate fanfare. Nevertheless, Sir Arthur Conan Doyle's character grew to become one of the world's most recognizable figures. Not only is Sherlock Holmes the most often-portrayed character in cinema, but his famous deerstalker hat and magnifying glass has made him as visually recognizable in the developing world as Napoleon, Adolf Hitler, and Jesus Christ.

As I have mentioned before, things which survive the test of time often have value beyond entertainment. Sherlock Holmes is not exception. Generations of schoolchildren and grandparents alike have learned how to reason through everyday problems by following Sherlock's example. Sherlock's method is elementary. First, Holmes gathers all of the available evidence—no matter how insignificant it may appear. Sherlock notes "it is a capital mistake to theorize before one has data. Insensibly one begins to twist facts to suit theories, instead of theories to suit facts".[61]

Once Holmes is in possession of the facts, he then "draws inferences from [his] observations."[62] These inferences are the first links in the chain of deductive logic which connect the crime's effect—a dead body—to its ultimate cause—the murderer himself. Finally, Holmes reminds himself to set aside his preconceptions, because if his logic is sound then "whatever remains, however improbable, must be the truth".[63]

The reader may notice that this book is structured like one of Sherlock Holmes' murder mysteries. I did this deliberately to not only to pay homage to Doyle, but because this structure makes it easy for casual readers to follow the "scarlet thread".

In Part 1 we explored the crime scene: we saw that millions of Americans are unemployed or underemployed, and that these numbers have been increasing for decades. Likewise, Americans today are worse off than their parents or grandparents. They cannot afford to eat steak for dinner. They cannot afford a house. They cannot afford to raise a family on a single income.

Worse still, the government has been hiding these facts with statistical chicanery and linguistic mumbo jumbo—they change definitions and compare apples to oranges, and paper over reduced purchasing power by distracting consumers with shiny new technology. A crime has been committed. America is bleeding out on the floor while her politicians and "experts" tiptoe around the body.

Our next step is to draw inferences from the evidence, and to use logic to deduce the ultimate cause. This is the subject of Part II. At the end of Chapter 4 we explored the offshoring vicious cycle. This is the murder weapon which broke America's back. In this Chapter, we will follow the scarlet thread and see how it ties America's economic problems to the trade deficit.

A STUDY IN SCARLET

As we noted in the prologue, America's GDP growth per person is the slowest it has been since the Great Depression. Between 2010 and 2015 it grew 0.147% on average, during the Great Depression, it grew 0.34% on average—twice as fast. These numbers have not improved. What is causing America's GDP to grow so slowly? In order to answer this question, we first need to understand how GDP works.

GDP is simply the value of all economic output—whether goods or services—produced in a specific area during a specific time period. GDP only includes the value of goods and services produced during the period. GDP does *not* include the value of things made in previous years, assets, nor the value of things expected to be made in later years, debt. Although assets and debts do not count towards GDP, they can still be exchanged for foreign production. This brings us to the other side of the equation: *consumption*.

National consumption is the value of everything purchased in a specific area during a specific time period. In a closed system, consumption always equals production in the long run—you cannot reap what you cannot sow. However, in an open system where entities can trade with one another, it is possible to consume more without making more. This is done by exchanging assets and debts. Although production and consumption must equal one another in the long run, in the short run they are subject variation. As usual, an example will clarify this point.

Sherlock Holmes and his loyal housekeeper, Mrs. Hudson, live at 221B Baker Street. Holmes produces detective consulting services worth £1,000 in 1887. Mrs. Hudson has also been busy, and produces £1,000 worth of fresh scones that year. As a result, we can say that Baker Street's "GDP" is £2,000 in 1887.

In a closed system—where residents of Baker Street were not allowed to trade with the outside world—Baker Street's consumption would also be £2,000. While there is little doubt Holmes would relish in his consulting, he would certainly grow tired of eating scones.

Luckily for Holmes—or more likely Mrs. Hudson—Baker Street is not a closed system. They have trade routes with Dr. Watson's office. In 1888 Holmes and Mrs. Hudson produce the same amount of output. However, Holmes also sells £500 worth of detective journals to Dr. Watson in exchange for his detective consulting services. Of course, Holmes could simply do this himself, but he would like to spend more time screeching on his violin. He also promises to pay Dr. Watson next year for an additional £500 worth of consulting. The good doctor obliges.

In 1888, although Baker Street's production remained £2,000 its consumption increased to £3,000. Baker Street could continue to consume more that it produces so long as Holmes finds more journals to sell and debt to promise. However, Baker Street cannot continue doing this indefinitely. Eventually, Holmes will need to solve £1,500 worth of mysteries a year, and pay Dr. Watson the extra £500 until his debt is paid. Over a long enough duration, production and consumption will always be equal.[v]

This logic explains how the trade deficit decreases America's GDP growth. In 2019 America's GDP was $21.43 trillion. On top of this, America

---

[v] The only exception to this rule is if Baker Street launched an invasion of Dr. Watson's office, and started stealing his pharmaceuticals with no reciprocal consideration. This is part of the reason that tribute has been mankind's modus operandi for generating long-term wealth throughout history. Bad trades can often be remedied at gunpoint.

bought a net $577 billion worth of goods and services from abroad, which is conveniently the value of the trade deficit in goods and services. As a result, America consumed $21.99 trillion worth of output in 2019.

If we assume that consumption, and not production, is the limiting economic factor, then we can safely say that the trade deficit *decreased* America's GDP by $577 billion in 2019. Likewise, it is also fair to say that the trade deficit has reduced America's cumulative GDP by up to $13.2 *trillion* since 2001. This logic only holds if we assume that if America stopped trading, production would rise to satisfy consumption, and not vice versa. Is this assumption reasonable? Yes.

OF FIVE ORANGE PIPS

If America were a closed system, there is good reason to believe that consumption—not production—would be the limiting factor. Why?

First, this has historically been the case. For most of its history America had extremely high tariffs which largely prohibited imports. Nevertheless, both GDP and national consumption grew well above the global average until America embraced global free trade. Likewise, free trade has not led to increased GDP growth—precisely the opposite occurred. The period of America's slowest economic growth correlates with the rise of its trade deficit.

Second, industrial production is subject to *increasing returns* on investment. We will explore this phenomenon in more detail in Chapter 8, but for now this basically means that the more we make of a product, the cheaper each unit of product becomes. For example, hand-built automobiles cost thousands at the turn of the Twentieth Century.

However, Henry Ford's Model T cost $850 once he had streamlined the factory process. Further, every Model T that Ford built decreased the average cost of production, because most of the costs were "fixed"—the factory cost the same price regardless of whether Ford made 100 cars or 10,000.

As a result, increasing returns helped drive the price down to $260 by 1924. The logic of increasing returns implies that at a certain level of consumption, the cost difference between American and Chinese goods would be negligible. Paradoxically, part of the reason that Americans find Chinese production cheap is because we are not producing enough ourselves. This may change in a system which discourages imports.

Third, Americans pay for the trade deficit by selling assets and promising debt. These financing options would remain open to Americans in a closed system, and therefore it is logical to assume that American consumers would continue to take full advantage of them. True, they may not get as much "bang for their buck", but that is a short-term problem. Ultimately, Americans are happy to spend as much as possible, no matter where the production originates.

Fourth, America is nowhere near its full production potential. In reality, tens of millions of Americans are unemployed, and many hundreds of billions worth of formerly productive assets are currently idle. America certainly has the economic spare capacity to increase production to match consumption, provided that the economic incentives were in place—or perhaps more appropriately, the disincentives were removed.

Essentially, America has spare production capacity, and it could quite easily be scaled-up to meet our own needs. America survived as a largely self-sufficient country for nearly two centuries, and could do so again.

Fifth, the desire to consume logically precedes the desire to produce—not vice versa. It is simply a truism that man makes because he wants. A hungry man will hunt, or fish, or farm. It is his desire to consume that drives his food production. It is not his love of reaping wheat or shucking corn that motivates his backbreaking labor. Work—production—is a means to an end. It is not the end itself.

The one major exception could be the production of art, but this exception proves the rule. Unsurprisingly, history is full of examples of nations finding ways to increase their production of various goods so that they could consume them. For example, Jamestown itself was created for the purposes of supplying England with tobacco.

Consumption drives production. In an open economic system—one where nations trade freely—it is possible to consume more than you produce. However, if the system were to close, we can deduce that production would rise to match consumption. Not vice versa.

This logic necessitates that the trade deficit displaces America's potential GDP: rather than build it, we buy it. Therefore, running a trade deficit *must* reduce GDP. This is the start of the scarlet thread upon which we will pull, which will unravel the mystery of America's economic decline.[vi]

THE REAPPEARING OF LADY FRANCES CARFAX

In Chapter 1 we explored the statistical shell game that is America's unemployment rate. We saw that although the BLS claimed the unemployment rate was just 3.5%—the lowest it has been in twenty years—the real unemployment rate is at least 7.5%. This is because the government considers many people without jobs as no longer being in the labor force. As a result, they were able to shrink the number of unemployed Americans from 12.2 million to 5.7 million.

---

vi It must be noted that although the trade deficit decreases GDP and retards economic growth, it is by no means the *only* factor. For example, high debt levels and low savings rate typically reduce investment, as do complex regulatory burdens, high taxes, and poor infrastructure. Although there are many anchors weighing-down America's economy, none are as pernicious as the trade deficit. This is because most of the other factors are themselves secondary heads stemming from the trade deficit's hydra. This will be explained in detail in Chapter 9.

On top of that, another 8 million Americans work part-time because they cannot find full time jobs. What's more, this statistical disappearing act has been going on for decades. America's labor force participation rate peaked in 2000 and it has been trending downward ever since. The data clearly shows that America's labor market is suffering.

The trade deficit is largely to blame for America's high unemployment. The logic is elementary. America produces and consumes. In a closed system, increased consumption drives increased production within the system—if Americans want more forks, they must make more forks.

In an open system, increased consumption still drives increased production, but this production may occur domestically or abroad. In this case, if America wants more forks, they can either make them or buy them from China. In essence, the trade deficit is the specter of America's offshore production—production which would occur in America in a closed system. [64]

The trade deficit reduces America's production, and the jobs needed to maintain that production. How many jobs does the trade deficit cost? Frankly, no one knows—and it is impossible to know. The economy is a complex system which cannot be measured in the same way that an astronomer measures the movement of the planets. At best we can speculate the extent of the job loss based on the economic data and historical precedent, similar to how a meteorologist estimates how much rain we can expect from a storm.

America's GDP was $21.4 trillion in 2019. Meanwhile, the trade deficit in goods was worth $846 billion, or 3.95% of GDP. Since GDP is the total output made by America's working population, and since 3.95% of America's GDP is displaced by offshore production, then it follows that roughly the same proportion of America's 158 million workers are likewise displaced by this offshore production.

If we assume that each offshored job is as productive as an American job, we can estimate that offshore production displaces 6.2 million American jobs. This is very similar to what we found in Chapter 1, where there are 6.5 million unemployed Americans whose existence are hidden by removing them from the labor force.

Let us tackle this problem another way. We know that manufactured goods constitute about 80% of America's trade deficit. This means we import approximately $677 billion worth of manufactured goods. Meanwhile, manufacturing makes up 11.39% of America's GDP, which is worth approximately $2.43 trillion. As such, we import just under one third of our manufactured goods. Given that manufacturing employed 12.8 million Americans to make $2.43 trillion in output, it stands to reason that we would need just over 4 million more workers to replace our imports.

In total, we can estimate that America would employ some 16.9 million Americans to manufacture enough goods to meet our consumption requirements. It is a not a coincidence that this figure is approximately the same as America's manufacturing employment figures from 2001—before the trade deficit seriously displaced America's GDP.

Our estimates have likely understated the true scope of job loss. Not all industries are created equal. Some are *anchor* industries, which make new wealth which support local economies. Examples of anchor industries are farms, mines, and factories.

Instead, most industries are *predicate* industries, whose existence usually depends upon the anchor industries. Examples of predicate industries include retail, restaurants, and professional services. Towns tend to develop around farms and factories, not retail outlets and restaurants. The line between anchor and predicate industries is sometimes blurred, but the distinction helps us forecast which industries support the economy more broadly.

As it turns out, manufacturing is the anchor industry which supports the most subsequent economic activity. This is because modern manufacturing is a complicated affair which requires many different materials and components from different suppliers. Therefore, manufacturing supports many different supply chains which form a complicated economic web.

Removing the key threads from this web—the factories themselves—causes the entire web to unravel. Economists have tried to quantify this, and estimate that each manufacturing job supports between 1.58 and 1.92 other predicate jobs.[65] Therefore, manufacturing job loss is just the frayed end of the scarlet thread. If we pull on the thread a little, we find that our 4 million lost manufacturing jobs would have supported between 6.32 and 7.68 million predicate jobs.

Overall, we can estimate that the trade deficit displaces between 6.2 and 11.7 million American jobs. Restoring these jobs would provide full-time work for millions of Americans, and would return America's unemployment rate back to its historical norms. Again, there are other factors that hurt America's labor market; however, the trade deficit is by far the most important element. In fact, if the trade deficit could be eliminated, this alone would be sufficient to resuscitate America's labor market.

OVER THE REICHENBACH FALLS

In Chapters 2 we saw how the American Dream is now unaffordable for the average American. We saw how real median wages stagnated in 1973, and how families are spending an ever-larger portion of their household income on needs as opposed to wants—breaking the economic trend which has marched inexorably forward from 1776 until 1985.

Not only are Americans today poorer than their parent's generation, but the true extent of poverty is also hidden through invisible inflation. Products which were once made of metal and lasted a decade, are now made of plastic and fall apart after a few years. Likewise, Americans have substituted nutrient-dense whole foods, like red meat and butter, for cheaper alternatives like chicken and palm oil. Although the trade deficit is not the only reason for this, it is likely the biggest factor.

Let us work backwards from this data—not unlike Sherlock Holmes—and see if we can deduce the killer of the American Dream. To begin with, wages stagnated in 1973. What is a wage? A wage is simply the price of labor, and like any other price, it is subject to the Laws of Supply and Demand.

In this context, the Law of Supply implies that decreasing supply increase prices, and increasing supply decreases prices. This explains why Pokémon cards with small supplies, like a Charizard, are expensive. Conversely, Pokémon cards with large supplies, like a Diglett, are not worth the paper they are printed on. The same goes for wages: physicians earn high salaries because there are very few physicians, whereas grocery store clerks earn small salaries because many people can scan groceries.

This logic walks hand-in-hand with the Law of Demand, which in this context implies that increased demand increases prices, and decreased demand decreases prices. For example, between 1634 and 1637 tulips became all the rage in Holland. The price of tulips—especially exotic-looking or novel flowers—increased exponentially. Some collectors paid up to 4,200 guilders for tulip bulbs. This worked out to 14 times the annual salary of a skilled craftsman. Increased demand increased tulip prices. Conversely, when tulip-mania ended, bulbs lost up to 99.99% of their value. Decreased demand decreased prices.

This logic likewise applies to wages. Increasing the labor supply will decrease wages. As we saw in Chapter 4, this is exactly what occurs in the off-shoring vicious cycle: when a factory closes the factory workers lose their jobs. Although most of them find new work, they increase the supply of labor and competition for other available jobs. In turn, this decreases the prices of labor, wages. When this is multiplied over *millions* of jobs, the effects are significant.

Real median wages peaked for American workers in 1973. America has run a trade deficit every year since 1974. This is not a coincidence. Ever since 1974 American jobs have been displaced by imports, and the number has been increasing year-over-year. Currently, the trade deficit destroys between 6.2 and 11.68 million jobs. This has increased the supply of labor and accordingly decreased wages.

Although the trade deficits' precise impact on wages is impossible to measure, we can deduce that just as it is sufficient to account for America's entire unemployment problem, it is likewise sufficient to account for America's entire wage stagnation problems. Additionally, research shows that when factory workers lose their jobs due to offshoring, their new jobs typically pay 17.5% less.[66] This is roughly in line with the amount of actual wage stagnation that we have witnessed.

Not only does the trade deficit decrease wages by directly increasing the labor supply, it does so indirectly by pitting American workers in competition with their counterparts in China and Mexico. Not all of America's factories have offshored. However, they all have the *option* to offshore if American workers become too expensive.

This breaks the backs of American unions, and individual workers, to negotiate better salaries and working conditions—why pay more to Americans when the Chinese will work for half the price? In this way, offshoring shifts bargaining power from workers to employers, which has provided a convenient pretext to decouple wages from productivity, which as we saw in Chapter 3, rose in lockstep up until 1973.

HIS LAST BOW

In Chapter 3 was explored the decaying of American industry. In 1979 over 19.5 million Americans worked in manufacturing. These jobs paid better than average, offered reasonable working hours, and usually offered pensions to their employees. By 2019 this number decreased to 11.7 million.

America has also lost the ability to mass manufacture products as basic, and strategic, as semiconductors—without which we cannot maintain our modern economy. To make matters worse, America manufactures fewer machine tools than Italy, which would mean that our road to economic self-sufficiency would be long and difficult. The trade deficit is self-evidently to blame for this issue.

As we have covered at length in earlier portions of this chapter, offshoring sufficiently accounts for America's manufacturing job loss. Likewise, it is obvious that moving almost all of our semiconductor factories to China makes it impossible for America to manufacture semiconductors, without first rebuilding the factories. This is immediately obvious, and we do not need to dwell on this point. The scarlet thread is visible and does not need to be further loosened.

That said, offshoring is not just today's problem, it is also tomorrow's problem. Why? Once a country loses the ability to produce something, it can be very difficult—if not practically impossible—to restart production of said product. This is because industrial development is largely *path-dependant*.

Path dependency means that the new builds on the old in a linear way, and different steps taken earlier in the process change the end result. Once you are on a path, you cannot easily switch to a different path. As usual, an example should clarify this.

There are two kingdoms, Holmesland and Mycroftia. Both kingdoms make 10 units clay pots and 10 units of copper tools per year. One day, someone in Holmesland invents the pottery wheel. The pottery wheel allows potters to spin their pots so that they can shape them faster. As such, Holmeslandian potters make pots twice as fast as they did before. The next year, Holmesland makes 20 units of clay pots.

Meanwhile, something similar happens in Mycroftia. That same year a mechanic invents the bellows, which is essentially a pump which feeds more air into a smelting fire. This allows the Mycroftians to smelt iron instead of copper, from which they can make iron tools that are twice as valuable. In both cases, the kingdoms' economies grew because they produced more economic value—more pots and more valuable tools.

The next year someone in Holmesland invents the flywheel. This allows potters to pump the pottery wheels with their feet, as opposed to spinning them by hand. Again, this makes potters twice as efficient. As such, Holmesland is able to build 40 units of clay pots. Likewise, Mycroftia invents the blast furnace, which delivers more fuel and air to the fire. This allows them to smelt steel, and make steel tools that are twice as valuable. In both cases economic growth stemmed from technological innovation.

Importantly, this second round of economic growth was path dependent. Why? Because the flywheel could not be invented—or even conceptualized—without the pottery wheel. Likewise, the blast furnace would not be possible to built without first inventing the bellows. This logic applies to all subsequent economic steps. Importantly, Holmesland and Mycroftia were on different industrial paths, and could not switch between paths without inventing or importing the preceding steps.

If industrial development is path dependent, then offshoring is akin to stepping off the path entirely. America has offshored a large portion of its industry abroad—particularly to China. As a result, the next steps in the industrial development are likely to occur in China. How can America benefit from the flywheel when we sent all of our potters wheels to China?

Is this not exactly what we have done with semiconductor manufacturing? The offshoring vicious cycle poses great economic risks, not only because it reduces our current GDP, but because it removes industries which may benefit from disruptive technologies in the future.

The trade deficit is America's scarlet thread of murder. It is woven into America's economic fabric, and is killing our GPD, our jobs, and our industries indiscriminately. Not only that, but it is poisoning our future economic growth. In Part I of this book, we observed the crime scene—America's economic problems. In this chapter we have draw inferences from the data, and deduced that the offshoring vicious cycle, which is reflected in the trade deficit, is the murder weapon.

In Part III we will see how free trade—often touted as the panacea to all economic maladies—is causing the trade deficit. Although this is contrary to what you may have learned in school and heard on the news, I urged you to approach the question of free trade with an open mind. Remember the words of Sherlock Holmes:

It is an old maxim of mine that when you have excluded the impossible, whatever remains, however improbable, must be the truth.[67]

CHAPTER 6

THE CURSE OF ATREUS, ON FREE TRADE'S NON-ECONOMIC HARMS

The sea was calm, and sun hot at Aulis. Agamemnon's ships were beachbound on the Aegean's shore, awaiting a wind to carry them to Troy. But Artemis cursed Mycenae's ambitious king with stagnant air. The oracle told Agamemnon that if he wanted wind, he must sacrifice his beloved daughter, Iphigenia, to the goddess Artemis. Agamemnon did so, and the winds spirited his fleet to the fabled walls of Ilium. Troy fell ten years later.

Agamemnon paid a terrible price for his glory, and yet, his penance had only begun. The murder of Iphigenia set in motion a series of events which would end Agamemnon's bloodline and destroy the House of Atreus. Upon his return to Greece, Agamemnon was murdered in his bathtub by his inconsolable wife, Clytemnestra. So too, his other children were haunted by the Furies—vengeful spirits—for their father's sins. His son Orestes was the last of his house.

The tragedy of Agamemnon reminds us that actions have unintended and unpredictable consequences. Just as Agamemnon sacrificed Iphigenia for wind, America has sacrificed much of its industrial might on alter of free trade. In exchange, politicians promised us "cheap" imported goods and better-paying jobs—wind to drive our economic growth.

As we saw in Chapters 1, 2, and 3, not only did America not receive what was promised, but the economic dislocation caused by free trade has set in motion a series of events which is destroying America. In this chapter we will tour some of non-economic consequences and dangers posed by America's trade deficit.

IN DEFENSE OF MARX

We have seen how the trade deficit destroys jobs, decreases wages, and increases the cost of living, impoverishing ordinary Americans. Meanwhile, multinational corporations have increased their profit margins by offshoring production to cheaper countries. Offshoring creates losers and winners, and therefore increases economic inequality.

Economic inequality is inevitable in a free market system: to the victor go the spoils. In fact, it is desirable because it provides a powerful economic incentive for people to "win" their economic competition—and the disincentive of losing is even greater. That said, the trade deficit has pushed economic inequality to dangerously high levels, levels which are threatening America's political stability.

The level of income inequality between countries can be compared by looking at their Gini-Coefficient ("GC"). A coefficient of "0" means that a country is perfectly equal, everyone earns the same income. Conversely, a coefficient of "1" means that a country is perfectly *un*equal, in that one individual earns all of the income.

Although GCs vary widely between countries, we observe that most politically stable countries have GCs between 0.25 and 0.4. For example, the GC of Canada, the Germany, and Japan all fall within this range. Meanwhile, countries above this range are much more likely to be political unstable. Examples include South Africa, Venezuela, and the Philippines. America's GC used to fall well within the "stability zone", however, it has been increasing since 1973. In the 1990s America's GC surpassed 0.4. Today, the GC respecting America's income is 0.48. This places America alongside countries like Guatemala and Brazil.

History teaches us that too much economic inequality leads to political instability. Consider the French Revolution. On July 14, 1789, Parisian insurgents stormed the Bastille, ushering in a new age of turmoil. Over the next five years King Louis XVI, along with hundreds of noblemen of ancient lineage, was decapitated.

Likewise, France's greatest cathedrals were seized by the Revolutionaries, and converted into Temples of Reason. Even the calendar months—which were unchanged since the reign of Caesar Augustus—were renamed. Soon thereafter, newly "liberated" France returned to authoritarianism under First Consul Napoleon Bonaparte. France was profoundly politically unstable.

One of the chief causes of France's instability was the vast disparity in wealth between the aristocracy and the peasants. On the one hand, the King lived in the exquisite Palace of Versailles. Meanwhile, peasants toiled day-in and day-out for their bread.

Edmund Burke, the godfather of Anglo-Saxon political conservatism, wrote in his *Reflections on the Revolution in France* that the Revolution was propelled by "men who knew nothing of the world beyond the bounds of an obscure village; who, immersed in hopeless poverty, could regard all property, whether secular or ecclesiastical, with no other eye than that of envy."[68]

Burke's sentiments were echoed by Karl Marx, who likewise opined that class inequality inevitably leads to bloody revolutions, and communism.[69] Both Burke and Marx recognized that humans indulge in envy. They covet their neighbour's silver, even when they sit on a throne of gold. Jealousy, or anger over a perceived unfairness—whether the unfairness is real or imaginary—drives men mad. It destabilizes society. It topples nations. In short, income inequality matters.

America's political stability is threatened by economic inequality. Consider that young people have been hit hardest by the trade deficit, as they lack the experience and connections to "win" in the job market. In fact, one in seven American men ages 20 to 24 do not work, are not enrolled in education, and are not training for future employment. They are "NEETs". The number is even higher for young women.[70] This is the greatest proportion of economically unproductive young people in America's history, and it is contributing to the rise in frequency, and the severity of political violence across the country.

For example, the death of George Floyd sparked protests across the country. Many of these protests turned violent—vandalism and looting were commonplace. Between May 26 and June 8, 2018, an estimated $2 billion in property was damage. Since then, violent protests, some bordering on insurrections, have become commonplace. For example, a portion of Seattle's Capitol Hill was occupied by protesters between June 8, 2020, and July 1, 2020. During this brief stint the Republic of CHAZ was declared, and like all communal "utopias" CHAZ was likewise taken over by a would-be warlord. Although these protests were not directly caused by the trade deficit, many of the most zealous protestors were NEETs enrolled in the ranks of Antifa.

This should come as no surprise. Individuals with no stake in society—with no skin in the game—are far more likely than people with jobs and children to engage in socially disruptive behavior. They have nothing to lose. In this way, the trade deficit has undoubtedly increased the frequency and size of these violent protests by increasing the number of NEETs and envious individuals. The trade deficit provided heap of kindling in need of a spark.

OSCAR WILDE'S WISDOM

When we talk about political instability, our mind immediately turns to protests and revolutions. However, the most commonplace and pernicious form of political instability is caused by big government, which tends to be more corrupt and political partisan. The trade deficit causes big government in two ways.

First, the trade deficit economically disadvantages millions of Americans, who are much more likely to elect socialist governments who promise to fix the problems. Remember, America's Rustbelt used to be a Republican political stronghold, and was swept by Presidents Dwight Eisenhower, Richard Nixon, and Ronald Reagan. However, as the region lost millions of jobs in the wake of NAFTA and China's admission to the WTO, the region turned blue.

Democrats promised that socialist policies could fix the economy, and insulate voters from the ravages of economic globalization. Of course, socialism did not deliver as promised. Instead, Democratic governments—at both the state and federal levels—were primarily successful in expanding the bureaucracy and increasing taxes and regulations.

Second, the trade deficit causes big government by providing a market for America's government to sell its debt. Remember, America funds the trade deficit by selling assets and promising to pay its debts. As such, a large trade deficit requires an equally large market for debt.

This allows America's government to borrow money from foreign governments at a relatively low rate of return—much lower than if they attempted to sell debt to the American public in a closed system. While lower interest rates may sound good, they simply incentivize the government to borrow more money. This allows the government to grow beyond the natural limitations imposed by tax revenues and domestic interest rates.

Big government destabilizes America in three main ways. First, big government wields more economic and political power than small government. This is a problem because governments concentrate important decisions in the hands of relatively few individuals. This amplifies the magnitude of any mistakes made by these decision makers.

Basically, it puts all of our eggs in one basket. On top of this, government decision makers—be they chief bureaucrats or the president—are more likely to make mistakes than are local stakeholders, because they are further removed from the consequences of their decisions, and may have ulterior political motives which distort their economic choices.

Second, big governments, like any large organizations, tend to be more corrupt. This is partly because people who are attracted to power and control gravitate towards organizations where they can obtain power and control. For example, estimates suggest that up to 12% of CEOs of major corporations exhibit psychopathic traits.[71] Conversely, there are very few psychopaths who choose to operate local mom-and-pop shops. Further, large scale organizations incentivize corruption by concentrating power while simultaneously diffusing accountability. It is very easy to play the blame game when you are a small cog in a big machine.

Finally, big government creates political instability by pitting the interests of citizens against one another. How so? Big governments hire more workers and provide welfare for more people. These workers then vote for bigger government so that they can secure their jobs or their handouts—very few people would vote to sacrifice their own interests for the common good.

Oscar Wilde summarized this process best with his famous quip: "the bureaucracy is expanding to meet the needs of the expanding bureaucracy".

Over time, this polarizes political parties and citizens into the *government party*, whose core constituents are government dependents, and the *populist party*, whose core constituents are people who do not rely on the government.

We saw this dynamic play out in the 2016 and 2020 election. Hillary Clinton and Joe Biden's political campaigns were primarily backed by America's plutocrats, government employees, white women, people of color, and recent immigrants. What links these massively disparate demographics together is that they all benefit from big government.

America's billionaires benefit because they can afford the lawyers and lobbyists necessary to navigate legislation which disadvantages smaller competitors. Likewise, government employees, women, people of color, and recent immigrants are all net recipients of government funding, whether through salaries or government benefits.

Meanwhile—as the media continuously reminds us—President Donald Trump was supported primarily by white males, who as a demographic pay more in tax than they receive in benefits. The misalignment of these demographic group's economic interests is a contributing factor towards their political divergence, and its destabilizing effect on America's political culture. And this misalignment is itself largely caused by the trade deficit.

LET THEM EAT CAKE!

Chronic unemployment caused by the trade deficit has also destabilized American society by increasing the rate of socially disruptive addictions, and undermining families. To begin with, the trade deficit has led to rampant drug abuse. Americans who are chronically unemployed are far more likely than average to be addicted to prescription and non-prescription drugs.

To some degree this is a chicken-and-egg problem: people with health issues may be less likely to work because of said issues; however, it has also been observed that unemployment tends to exacerbate underlying health issues. For example, retirement increases the likelihood of fatality in men by a significant degree, regardless of their retirement age.[72]

In any case, the fact is that the number of Americans on prescription medications for depression and chronic pain has been increasing since 1973, largely in lockstep with the growth of the trade deficit. Presently, some 13.2% of Americans took antidepressant medications within the last 30 days.[73] Likewise, 10.7% of Americans used prescription painkillers in the last 30 days.[74]

Unsurprisingly, more people taking prescription drugs has led to more people becoming addicted to their prescription drugs, and more overdoses. In 2019 over 70,000 Americans died from drug overdoses. The vast majority of those deaths were caused by prescription opioids.[75] It is unlikely that these people would have been set down the path of addiction, were it not for the economic disasters caused by the trade deficit. It is not an understatement to say that the trade deficit is killing tens of thousands of Americans every single year.

Economic hopelessness also leads to pornography addiction. Although this is very seldom discussed, pornography addiction is the *most common* form of addiction for men. In fact, studies estimate that some 10% of men are addicted to pornography.[76] This addiction has dire consequences for both addicts and society.

As Gary Wilson describes in his book *Your Brain on Porn*, frequent viewing of pornography physically alters the brain's structure, rewiring neuropathways and desensitizing dopamine receptors to such a degree that a pornography addict's brain is largely indistinguishable from the brain of a heroin addict.

On top of this, pornography addiction leads to physical and psychological impairments like erectile dysfunction, lower testosterone levels, and social anxiety and depression. Again, the link between the trade deficit and the rise in pornography addiction is tenuous, but logical. Men with jobs are less likely to engage in addictive behaviors, whether drugs or pornography.

Finally, the trade deficit destabilizes society by hurting families. It hurts families in two main ways. First, chronic unemployment, wage stagnation, and a high cost of living has led to Americans forming fewer families, and these families likewise have fewer children. Second, the have caused more families to break apart. To begin with, fewer Americans are getting married and having children than ever before. Although social considerations have played a large role in this—in particular the widespread use of contraception—the biggest factor remains the economy.

On a statistical level, women are sexually attracted to men who earn more money than them, and will typically refuse to marry men who earn less than them. Likewise, regions in which women earn more than men on average have fewer marriages than regions where men earn more than women.[77] Because the trade deficit has resulted in the offshoring of jobs typically worked by males—manufacturing being the most obvious example—women under the age of 35 now earn more than men of the same age, once variables such as experience and hours worked are accounted for. This is a recipe for dysfunctional marriages.

On top of this, most families have fewer children than they would prefer. Survey data shows that the overwhelming reason for this is a poor economy. For example, of families who had fewer children than they would have liked, 64% said that expensive childcare was a consideration. Meanwhile 49% cited a bad economy, 44% said they could not afford more children, and 43% said they waited too long due to financial instability. In total, four of the top five answers were economic in nature.[78] America's poor economy is harming the formation of families, and depressing the nation's birth rate.

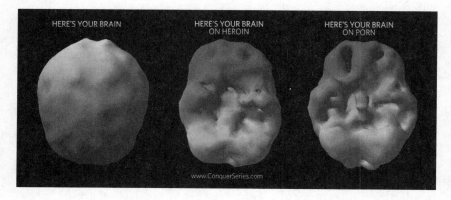

On the other side of the coin, economic problems are the number one reason why married couples divorce, and unmarried couples separate. This has led to a surging divorce rate, and an increasingly large number of children living in "blended" families.

Children raised in such families are significantly more likely to suffer from physical and psychological health problems. They perform worse academically.[79] They are significantly more likely to engage in criminal behaviors.[80] Interestingly, divorce reduces future productivity growth of heads of households—usually the fathers—by 25%.[81] That is, divorce causes tangible economic damage, which makes future divorces even more likely. It is a vicious cycle that only really benefits divorce lawyers like me.

To tie everything together: the trade deficit destroys jobs, reduces wages, and increases the cost of living. Young people are disproportionately affected by the trade deficit, since low-level jobs are the first to be offshored. Unsurprisingly, America's disaffected youth have destabilized America's social fabric by rioting, or becoming addicted to drugs and pornography.

To make matters worse, the trade deficit has distorted the economy in such a way that people are less likely to form families and have children, and those that do are more likely to go through a divorce. In turn, this social instability further damages the economy, and the vicious cycle repeats.

Our economy and our society cannot be understood in isolation from one another: economic problems have social consequences, and social problems have economic consequences. Modern economists have promoted free trade agreements like NAFTA on the grounds that they will have broad economic benefits, cheaper goods for everyone, at the expense of geographically concentrated economic harms, job loss in Michigan.

The problem with this approach is that we are not just causing economic harms. We are causing social harms which destabilize society, destroy families, and kill people. This anguish radiates throughout America and reverberates across generations. And what is the government's answer to the plight of middle America?

In the words of Marie Antoinette—shortly before she was beheaded—"Let them eat cake".

LAMENT FOR A NATION

Aside from King John's *Magna Carta* and Emperor Justinian's *Corpus Juris Civilis*, the *Treaty of Westphalia* is perhaps the most important legal document in Western history. This is not because it ended the gruesome Wars of Religion, laying the political foundations for the Age of Enlightenment, but because it redefined the notion of sovereignty and created the modern nation-state.

The Treaty affirmed, for perhaps the first time since the fall of Rome, that a nation has supreme authority within its borders—to the exclusion of supranational organizations like the Catholic Church or the Holy Roman Empire.

This specific, and new, notion of sovereignty has been the modus operandi for political thinkers ever since, and it is this type of sovereignty that conservatives seek to protect from international organizations like the United Nations ("UN") or the European Union ("EU"). In order for an international entity to function, each member state must surrender specific powers—a piece of their sovereignty—to said entity. This is not necessarily bad. For example, most countries agree to respect each other's territorial integrity, otherwise they risk international action. However, this is a slippery slope.

Consider the EU's actions during the 2015 European Debt Crisis. The EU appointed a special counsel, known as the Troika, to reign-in Greece's spending and reduce their debt burden. Of course, controlling Greece's finances meant controlling Greece itself: the elections were nullified, and the Troika violated the peoples' property rights to prop-up Greece's big banks. This was an egregious overstep, wherein a sovereign nation was essentially occupied without a shot being fired.

In spite of this, conservatives are paradoxically the strongest advocates of free trade and economic globalization—which also sap national sovereignty. Remember, in order for nations to trade freely, they must harmonize their laws and regulations respecting whatever goods or services they seek to trade. This necessarily results in a loss of national sovereignty. For example, up to 75% of Great Britain's laws and regulations were changed so as to comply with EU common market protocols.[82] These laws were not made by accountable politicians in Britain, but by faceless men in Brussels.

The same process occurred when America entered into NAFTA with Canada and Mexico. The three nations harmonized their regulations so that they could facilitate free trade. Due to America's economic clout, Canada and Mexico largely modified their own regulations to comply with those in America.

However, imagine if America wanted to enter into a free trade agreement with the European Union. In this case, America would be the junior economic partner, and it seems likely that America's laws would be harmonized with Europe's—it seems plausible that America would adopt the metric system, but impossible that Europe would re-adopt the imperial system.

History teaches us that economic unification eventually leads to political unification. In fact, the process is so inevitable that it even occurred in Greco-Roman Antiquity. For example, Rome assimilated the states of Latium not primarily through violence, but through trade and economic integration. Rome was the largest city in Latium, and as a result Roman culture and standards were adopted through the region, and not vice versa. Over time, the distinctions between Romans and other Latians disappeared to the point that only Romans remained.

On the other side of the Mediterranean, the Delian League—a loose alliance Greek city-states—was rapidly transformed into the Athenian Empire. At first the League established a common treasury on the Island of Delos. So too, the League harmonized trade policies. As the largest city, Athenian norms were adopted by the League. Over time, Athens' economic clout was leveraged into political clout. The treasury was moved to Athens, and voluntary contributions became tributary taxes.

A more recent example of this process occurred with the evolution of the EU. The EU's foundations were laid with the creation of the European Coal and Steel Community in 1952, a trade agreement that harmonized supply chains of said critical resources. Not only would it be economically expedient, it was marketed by its architect Robert Schuman in 1950 as something that would "make war materially impossible." From the beginning, European technocrats realized that economic integration would inevitably lead to political integration.

History proved them right. Trade agreement after agreement followed, each justified on economic grounds, and supported by conservatives—who could say no to free trade or to the prosperity it promised? And perhaps the EU did enrich Europe, but at what cost?

A single market requires a single law: European nations sacrificed their political independence upon the altar of economic interdependence. Europe now shares an increasingly powerful legislature, single currency, and constitution—and if the EU's architects have their way, Europe will once again have a Caesar. America should take heed.

A DRAGON FED

The Second Amendment guarantees the right of every American citizen to bear arms. Generations of conservative politicians and thinkers have argued that this right is our *most important* constitutional right. Why? Our other constitutional rights, like free speech, are worthless unless they can be protected. Firearms safeguard freedom.

Interestingly, those same politicians and thinkers often ignore the trade deficit. This is foolish. The trade deficit is perhaps the greatest international threat to America's freedom, posing three main risks. First, America's dependence upon foreign imports limits our ability to act independently and defend our nation. Second, asymmetrical trade with our rivals enriches them at our expense. Third, the type of economic integration embodied in the trade deficit increases the likelihood of international conflict.

The trade deficit undermines America's national security because of something called *import dependency*. Import dependency occurs when a country cannot sustain itself without imports. This often occurs when countries lack a specific natural resource.

For example, Germany relies almost entirely upon Russia to supply its oil and natural gas. No Russian oil, no German economy. The national security threats posed by Germany's reliance on Russian petrochemicals is immediately obvious: Germany must consider Russian political interests when making its own policy decisions, as upsetting the bear could have dire economic consequences. Further, Germany's ability to resist Russian military aggression is severely compromised by its reliance upon Russian fuel. Should a conflict erupt,

Russia could simply turn off the taps and watch Germany's military grind to a halt.

We have seen premonitions of this in the 2022 Russo-Ukraine War. Russia has used Europe's import dependency respecting Russian oil to mitigate Europe's opposition to its invasion of the Ukraine. Further, Russia was also able to neuter the Ukrainian resistance by denying their access to fuel. Europe's import dependency is a clear and present danger which no serious scholar denies.

Less obvious, however, is the threat posed by dependence upon foreign manufactured goods. The best historical example of this dependence occurred during the American Revolution. Although this may come as a surprise, the American Revolution almost failed because the Colonies could not manufacture enough cannons, firearms, and gunpowder to resist the British—our former supplier.

It was only when Britain's European rivals, particularly the French and Dutch, started supplying the Revolutionary Army that the tide turned. For example, France alone supplied the Revolutionary Army with over 80,000 firearms, in addition to swords, knives, and uniforms.[83] America depended upon British manufactured goods, and it was not until this economic dependence was broken that America could free herself from the imperial yoke.

President George Washington recognized this fact, writing that America would not be able to defend its freedoms unless the nation was "independent of others for essential, particularly military, supplies". To this end, his first major piece of legislation was the *Tariff Act* of 1789, which raised taxes on imported manufactured goods.

One of the legislation's key aims was to promote the development of America's manufacturing industry. Even Thomas Jefferson—who initially supported free trade on principle—eventually agreed with Washington. In the wake of the War of 1812, Jefferson wrote:

> ...*experience has taught me that manufactures are now as necessary to our independence as to our comfort: and if those who quote me as of a different opinion will keep pace with me in purchasing nothing foreign where an equivalent of domestic fabric can be obtained, without regard to difference of price [we would be well-off]...*

Both Washington and Jefferson realized that economics and politics are simply two sides of the same coin. Therefore, to safeguard America's political independence, she must first maintain her economic independence.

In Chapter 3 we learned that America now imports nearly $500 billion worth of advanced technology products every year. Likewise, America's industrial base has been hollowed-out to the point where we depend upon imported machine tools and semiconductors—never mind more innocuous goods like cutlery and baseball caps.

America is import-dependent upon China. This restrains America's ability to act independently on the world stage, and gives China leverage over America in any prospective military engagement.

Consider what would occur if conflict erupted between America and China. Presumably, America would need to scale-up its industrial production to build more weapons, vehicles, and computers. There is just one problem: scaling-up is just not possible—at least not immediately. Why?

In order to manufacture more equipment, America would need to build more factories. However, America imports almost all of its industrial components and machine tools. That is, America does not even manufacture the things it would need to use to manufacture more things.

Worse yet, America's workforce lacks the training and experience to manufacture critical goods. What would happen, for example, if China stopped selling microchips? Even if we assume that America has the tools to manufacture microchips—which we do not—we do not have the human capital to manufacture microchips on a large scale. That is, very few Americans know how to build microchips. Heck, very few Americans even have the skills to build the factories themselves.

This brings me to my next point: America's economy is a sham. On paper, America's economy is the largest in the world. In 2022 our nominal GDP was $26.9 trillion. Meanwhile, China's economy was a distant second, with a nominal GDP of just $19.4 trillion. This means that America produced over $7 trillion most output than China. Not bad right? Wrong.

These numbers are misleading because they compare apples to oranges. Thanks to inflation, a dollar can buy quite a bit more in China than in America. Therefore, a more useful comparison is to look at the *purchasing power parity* of each country. If we do this then America's GDP remains the same, since it is our baseline. However, China's GDP balloons to $33 trillion. That is, China actually produced $6 trillion *more* than America.

To make matters worse, not all economic output is the same. America's economy looks big because we produce many valuable services. That is, much of our GDP is created by Wall Street banks and Silicon Valley technology companies.

The problem is that much of this "wealth" is just an illusion. For example, studies have estimated that Americans pay financial services providers over $400 billion per year simply to file their taxes. This "creates wealth" in the sense that it increases GDP—but can any sane person say that these financial services actually make Americans richer? More importantly, could we rely on this GDP during a war? No.

When we compare America and China in terms of our *productive* economic sectors—how much physical output like food, manufactured goods, new buildings we make—the picture is even more bleak. In 2022 services accounted for 80.2% of America's GDP. This means that America produced just $5.3 trillion worth of physical output. Meanwhile, just 52.3% of China's GDP was services, and a whopping 33.2% of its economy was industrial output. In total, China's productive economy was $15.7 trillion—three times larger than America's.

America may have a large legacy military, but the nation is essentially running on fumes. There is little doubt that China's astute leadership recognizes this fact, and they may be willing to use their economic leverage over America in the same way that Russia has used its leverage over Europe to gobble up the Crimea and the eastern provinces of the Ukraine. And based on the size of China's economy, there is very little we could do about it.

The trade deficit also threatens America by enriching our rivals. Economists argue that free trade between nations benefits both nations, albeit at different rates. For example, America's economy benefits from importing cheap Chinese goods: in theory, these imports make America's economy more efficient, and offshoring frees American workers to focus their efforts on making higher-margin products. Likewise, China has benefited from importing American technology, and building factories to service America's large consumer market.

Even if we assume that both America and China benefit from this trade relationship, there is no question that China has benefited *more* than America. Just consider that China's economy has grown by an average of 8% per year since opened for trade. Meanwhile, it is debatable whether America's economy has grown whatsoever in real terms, after accounting for population growth and technological change.

From an economic standpoint, there is no issue with asymmetrical trade relationships. However, this is a big political problem. Power is zero-sum. As China grows in wealth it grows in power. A powerful China poses a threat to America. This is not to say China would invade America—China has been one of the world's most peaceful nations historically. However, a powerful China provides America's satellite states and trading partners with a credible alternative modality. America has benefited enormously from being the "only game in town" after the fall of the USSR. China's rise is upsetting this unipolar dynamic, which indirectly harms America's ability to project its self interest.

Lastly, the trade deficit represents increased economic integration between America and the rest of the world. History shows us that economic integration not only makes America vulnerable, but it also increases the likelihood of conflict. This is because more interactions multiplies the number of political tensions that could escalate into violence.

Consider the fact that almost every historical war was fought between nations with close economic links. Further, the more they traded, the more they fought. For example, the Spanish Empire and the Netherlands fought the brutal Eighty Year's War primarily because the Spanish Empire could not afford to relinquish the territories—direct taxation of the Netherlands was the only way the Spanish crown could mitigate the impact of their enormous trade deficit with the Netherlands.

Conversely, economic isolation typically walks hand-in-hand with peace. For example, until Commodore Matthew Perry opened Japan for trade, the island was profoundly uninterested in foreign wars. In the following decades, Japan modernized, and as it did so its economy became increasingly dependent on foreign resources, like oil and rubber. This led to the expansion of the Japanese Empire. The same was largely true of China until the 1980s and the United States until the Second World War.

Import dependency is America's golden shackles. It limits America's ability to act independently, and undermines our national security—one cannot fight their own supplier. Further, the trade deficit has enriched China at America's expense, and as such we have created ourself a new rival. America would have been far safer had we paid more for domestic goods and left China to wallow in the medieval ages.

Finally, the trade deficit is a product of economic globalization, and it multiplies the flashpoints that could lead to armed conflict. Most wars between great powers are fought over tiny spits of land that are not themselves very important, such Serbia in World War I and the Polish Corridor in World War II.

If America was serious about preserving its national security, reigning in the trade deficit would be our top priority.

TURTLES ALL THE WAY DOWN

On January 28, 1986, the space shuttle Challenger exploded. All seven astronauts were killed. Eyewitness Frank Mottek described the scene:

> *Just then we both stood up and looked up at the shuttle making its way farther and farther into the sky. Suddenly, I was struck by a pattern I had never seen before. From our vantage point, it appeared that an extra flame was trailing from the shuttle. Then, in that split second, a silent fireball appeared in the sky. Then there was silence, the silence of alarm...*

Investigations later revealed that two rubber O-rings, which were designed to separate the sections of the rocket booster, failed. Rather than remaining supple, they cracked because of cold temperatures. Pressurized fuel escaped through the crack, ignited, and exploded. The Challenger is America's Titanic, our Hindenburg. It is a disaster forever burned into our national consciousness.

We have already forgotten the Challenger's lesson: the whole is only as strong as its weakest part. Perhaps this sounds trite. But sometimes the simplest observations are the most consequential. In this case, trillions of dollars—if not America's economic future—depends on understanding how O-rings fail.

In 1993, Michael Kremer, a Harvard-educated developmental economist, wrote a paper called "The O-Ring Theory of Economic Development". For Kremer, the Challenger disaster was not just a tragedy, it was also a parable that helped explain why workers in some countries and industries earn exponentially more than workers in other countries and industries, despite doing basically the same job. It all comes down to fragility and exponents. An example will clarify how this process works.

Imagine that you own a factory making glass vases. It takes two workers to make one vase: one worker blows the molten glass, the other packs the vase for delivery. If either worker drops the vase, it will shatter and become worthless. You have four workers. Two of them never drop the vase. Two of them drop it half the time. If you want to make as many vases as possible, how should you divide your workers?

Instinct tells us to pair the good and bad workers—that way both teams will have someone who knows what they're doing, and both will be somewhat successful. This is a bad idea. If you did this, then both teams would break 50 percent of the vases. The better option is to pair the good workers together and let the bad workers make a mess. Why? Together the good workers would succeed 100 percent of the time. Meanwhile, the bad workers would succeed 25 percent of the time. On average, the teams would succeed in making vases 62.5 percent of the time. The second option is the clear winner.

This example highlights two important lessons. First, vase production is *fragile*—one small mistake at any point in the production-chain can destroy the whole vase. The chain is only as strong as its weakest link. Second, increasing the production chain's complexity, by adding an extra step, will increase the fragility in a non-linear way. How?

Imagine that you also need to paint the vases, adding a third step. Although your two good workers succeed 100 percent of the time, they are forced to work with butterfingers, who drops the vase half the time. In this case, the entire

121

factory's productivity decreases from 62.5 to 50 percent. Now pretend that you also need to varnish the vases, adding a fourth step. Your final employee is also a dropper, and decreases the factory's output to 25 percent.

Now pretend that it takes 100 steps to make a vase: you have 97 employees who succeed 100 percent of the time, and just three bad employees (who succeed 50 percent of the time). In this case, the factory's production efficacy would *decrease* to just 12.5 percent—despite the fact that you hired an army of competent workers! When it comes to O-ring economics, one bad apple really does spoil the bunch.

The above logic has profound implications for America's trade policy— implications that America's economic stewards completely ignore. To begin with, offshoring adds complexity, as in extra steps to the production chain, which increases the likelihood that something will go wrong. And remember, this complexity harms production in a non-linear way—even a small failure in an otherwise flawless production chain can destroy the entire product.

Technologically sophisticated output is especially vulnerable. For example, Boeing's 787 Dreamliner suffered numerous delays, cost-overruns, and safety problems because the international supply chain was too complex. Consider that Boeing employed some 50 different contractors, each of whom was responsible for designing and manufacturing a piece of the airplane.[84] Complicating things further was the fact that these contractors often sub-contracted their production. And no doubt these sub-contractors further sub-contracted their work. This is the economic equivalent of the Hindu's infinite regression: subcontractors all the way down.

God only knows how many different companies, located in how many different countries, worked on the 787. Rather than building an airplane, Boeing was building a puzzle with pieces of obscure provenance. Basically, Boeing had no idea if it was employing "vase-droppers" until it was too late. The fact that things have not gone wrong for America on an apocalyptic level is largely due to the fact that American companies have hired legions of business consul-tants, logistics engineers, and risk-managers to "streamline" international supply chains. In fact, the growth of America's managerial class is largely a response to offshoring and to the burden of increasing complexity.

Economists *never* account for the cost of this additional management when they discuss offshoring. Instead, the existence of a bloated managerial class is simply taken for granted. This raises the question: are Chinese goods cheap, or do they *appear* cheap because we ignore the opportunity costs associ-ated with employing millions of Americans in non-productive jobs? How many millions of man-hours do we waste coordinating the labor of Chinese peasants? How many more are wasted coordinating the coordinators? America is sac-rificing its productive human capital on the altar of complexity: we trade the wisdom of makers for the trickery of takers.

Complexity is not just an economic problem, it's an existential threat. In his book *The Collapse of Complex Societies*, Joseph Tainter argues that civiliza-tions collapse because they can no longer maintain their level of organizational, economic, and technological complexity. Increasing complexity is driven by an autocatalytic process—as societies grow, they require more organization, which enables them to grow bigger still etc. Eventually, society becomes too compli-cated to survive with the available technology. Collapse becomes inevitable.

Symptoms of an impending collapse often include the expansion of bureaucracies—bureaucrats being loosely defined as "organizers" rather than "producers"—increased taxes to pay for said bureaucracies, the proliferation of laws, increasing debt, currency debasement, widening economic inequality, and the consolidation of capital (land) ownership. You do not have to be Tiresias to see that America—if not Western Civilization itself—is nearing a complexity-driven collapse.

Our bureaucracy is bloated: over 22 million Americans work for the government, twice the number that work in manufacturing, and more than

60% of Americans receive government subsidies. The majority of Americans are de facto wards of the state. Ours is a nation of takers, not makers. If America is going to survive and prosper, we *must* simplify the economy. Otherwise, we will crash and burn for want of an O-ring.

O BONNY PORTMORE, I AM SORRY TO SEE / SUCH A WOEFUL DESTRUCTION...

As the hysteria over "global warming" heats up, carbon taxes have become the cool option—and not just for environmentalists and greedy politicians, but allegedly level-headed economists as well. For example, a 2017 report penned by 13 leading economists, including two Nobel Prize winners, recommends that countries work together to institute a global carbon tax. The paper argues that doing so would help price out carbon-intensive industries and reduce pollution.[85]

What environmentalists forget is that America's economy is not a closed system: rather than follow America's environmental regulations, big polluters can simply move their operations to places like China, India, or the Philippines. In this sense, America's trade deficit is a measure of how much pollution our nation has exported to the Third World—pollution which eventually returns to us in the form of acid rain, putrid air, and poison food.

First, we will look at the trade deficit's impact on carbon emissions. To be clear, carbon dioxide ("CO2") is not itself a form of atmospheric pollution. Humans inhale oxygen and exhale CO2. Likewise, plants "inhale" carbon dioxide and "exhale" oxygen. CO2 is, quite literally, the breath of life. Further, plants grow faster when there is more CO2 in the environment, which is why greenhouses and aquariums increase ambient CO2 levels to boost crop yields. Most environmentalists claim that CO2 is a pollutant because it is a "greenhouse gas" which helps traps solar radiation in the atmosphere, therefore heating the earth.

These arguments are easily dismantled in three ways. First, earth's climate is a *complex system*, and therefore it is impossible for us to predict with certainty how CO2 levels interact with temperature. This argument will be fleshed out in Chapter 7, when I discuss complex systems in relation to the economy.

Second, the dataset purporting to tell us that the planet is warming is too small to draw any rational conclusions. The Law of Large Numbers states that as a sample size increases, the mean average of said sample becomes closer to the mean average of the whole population. We have been accurately measuring "global" temperatures for just a few decades. Before that, almost all measurements came from either Europe or North America.

Further, most temperature readings come from places where people live. There are relatively few samples from the oceans, which cover 70% of the globe, or from sparsely populated or uninhabited areas, which account for 60% of our land masses. Given that earth's climate fluctuates on cycles which take tens of thousands of years, and our quality samples are limited to tens of years, it is hubristic to assume we really know what is going on.

Third, if CO2 causes global warming there appears to be no cause for alarm. Even if global temperatures rise by a degree or two, this difference pales between those regional climatic differences between places like Maine and Florida—both of which support human life equally well. We note that paleontologist estimate CO2 levels were over 10 times higher in the dinosaur era than they are today.[86] Evidently this was *good* for life on earth, both in terms of overall organic mass and in terms of biodiversity.

Although CO2 is not itself a pollutant, CO2 emissions from industrial processes are often laced with actual pollutants such as sulfur dioxide or nitrogen oxides which cause acid rain, or various particulate matter which causes smog and poisons plants, animals, and humans. As a result, we can use CO2 as a proxy to track more harmful forms of pollution. The data unequivocally shows that America's trade deficit has not only increased global pollution levels, but that our own environmental regulations have done more harm than good.

To begin, data from the World Bank reveals that China, and other Third World countries, produce far more carbon per dollar of economic output than do Western nations. For example, China produced 0.6kg of CO2 per dollar of economic output in 2014. Conversely, America produced just 0.3kg of CO2 for the same amount of economic output. European countries like German produced even less.[87] This means that every factory that moves from Ohio to Shenzhen will at least *double* the emissions of said factory.

The offshoring reflected in America's trade deficit, which catalyzed China's economic development, is to blame for the dramatic rise in emissions over the last two decades. The below graph makes this clear.

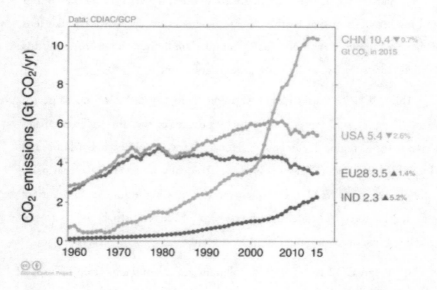

Not only has the trade deficit increased global emissions by fueling China's growth, but it has undermined America's attempts to reduce emissions. The economy is not a closed system. When confronted with onerous environmental regulations, many American companies simply relocate their operations abroad.

As a result, environmental regulations and carbon taxes have the ultimate effect of actually *increasing* America's emissions by replacing relatively clean American factories with "dirty" Chinese factories. This is not a secret. A paper published in the *Proceedings of the National Academy of Sciences* found that the CO2 reductions allege by the Kyoto Protocol were more than offset by emissions from goods imported from China.[88]

Of course, emissions are not the only form of pollution. Consider that some 1.6 million square kilometres of the Pacific Ocean, an area roughly twice as large as Texas, is now covered by a floating blanket of plastic debris. Although most the plastic particles are microscopic, they are causing massive harm to earth's ecosystems. Plastic eaten by sea creatures is also winding up in human bodies.

Plastic pollution is affecting the health of our children, and could endanger the existence of humanity itself. In 2020 microplastics were found incorporated into the tissue of human placentas for the first time, indicating that newborn babies may be partially composed or inorganic tissue.[89] While the long-term health consequences of being partially composed of plastic are not known, one can assume that they are not good.

In any case, almost all of the plastics and microplastics which are dumped in the world's oceans come from Asia—not America, Europe, or any other region which the *World Economic Forum* and environmentalists blame for the world's pollution problems. In fact, 80.99% of all plastic dumped into the ocean as of 2019 came from Asia.

The biggest culprit was the Philippines, which emitted 36.38% of all oceanic plastic in 2019. This is compared to 12.92% for India, 7.22% for China, and 0.25% for America.[90] You read that right. The Philippines emits 145 times more plastic into the world's oceans than does the entire USA. Every factory that moves from America to the Third World is an environmental tragedy of absurd proportions.

America's environmental track record is not spotless. In fact, Americans pollute more per person than most of our cousins in Europe, Canada, and Australia. However, there is a world of difference between America's environmental impact and that of developing countries like China, India, or the Philippines.

If America's leftist were serious about protecting the environment, they would not focus on carbon taxes or banning plastic drinking straws. Instead, they would focus on reducing America's trade deficit, which more than offsets all of the "progress" we have made at home.

IN MEMORIAM OF JOHN BULL

The trade deficit kills jobs and reduces wages. As we have seen, American families spend more on wants than needs now than they did in 1984. We also witnessed that invisible inflation has forced Americans to make dietary substitutions, which have become culturally justified as being "healthier".

In general, Americans have moved from eating diets rich in nutritious animal products to plant-based diets. This dietary transition is at the root of why so many Americans today are obese yet malnourished. In this way, the trade deficit makes us physically unhealthy.

The most significant dietary substitution occurred when Americans stopped cooking with animal fats, like butter and lard, and started cooking with plant-derived fats, like shortening and margarine. This substitution was mostly motivated by cost concerns. For example, in 1911 B&G Foods brought Crisco to market.

Crisco is made from cottonseed oil. Prior to its use as a food, cottonseed oil was generally regarded as a waste product, and in cases when it was used it ended up as an industrial lubricant or an ingredient in cosmetics and detergents. That said, cottonseed oil did have one thing going for it: it was cheap. Although seed and vegetable oils, like Crisco, were marketed as being "healthy" alternatives to animal fats, the American public was reticent to eat them until the 1970s, when incomes stagnated. Today, vegetable fats have almost completely usurped traditional animal fats in American diets.

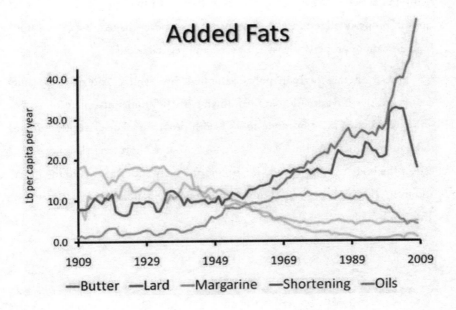

Added Fats

Lb per capita per year

—Butter —Lard —Margarine —Shortening —Oils

Most fats derived from vegetables and seeds are synthetic products, which undergo extensive processing to turn them from inedible industrial products into allegedly edible food products. For example, rapeseed oil is made in the following way. First, rapeseeds are heated to relatively high temperatures so that they oxidize, which makes them rancid and completely inedible.

Next, this sludge is processed with petroleum solvents to extract the oils. The oily sludge is then heated again, and acid is removed to remove any waxy solids which may have formed. The remaining is oil is then chemically treated and deodorized to improve its color and scent—without these final processes this "food" would be completely inedible. This is very different than the processing of traditional vegetable fats such as olive oil, which is simply cold-pressed, or animal fats like butter, which is easily churned from fresh cream.

Vegetable and seed oils are at the root of many of America's health problems. The main reason for this is that the human body has evolved over many millennia to digest certain types of foods. In the same way that ducks cannot properly digest bread—because ducks never baked bread—so too humans cannot properly digest most seed and vegetable oils.

These oils are high in polyunsaturated fats, which oxidize easily and cause excessive inflammation in the human body. Chronic inflammation is the ultimate cause of most of modernity's health problems. For example, chronic inflammation increases the levels of cortisol, the "stress" hormone. This hormone causes the body to store visceral fat around the belly and organs, like the heart and liver. This leads to health problems like obesity, diabetes, and heart disease. This is made obvious in the graphs below:

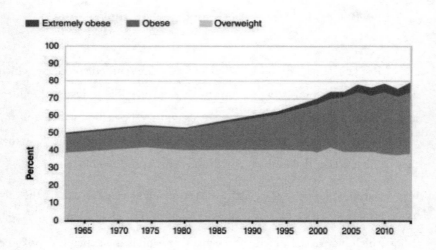

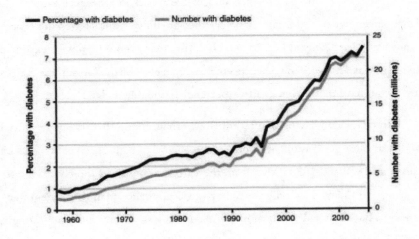

Likewise, excess cortisol dampens the function of the human immune system, which is responsible for suppressing the growth of cancers and infectious diseases. This partly explains why the incidence of cancer has increased by nearly 30% since 1973.[91] Finally, cortisol is inversely related with other hormones like testosterone and human growth hormone. This has had a profound affect on men's health in America.

Consider that sperm counts have decreased by 59% between 1973 and 2011.[92] Further, average male testosterone levels have been declining by about 1% per year since the same period.[93] This has obviously implications not only for human fertility, but the functioning of society itself. Testosterone is the "male" hormone, and it plays an important role in motivating men to engage in competitive, creative, pro-social behaviors. As we will see in Chapter 8, these are the very sorts of behaviors that are key to driving economic growth.

At this point, it should go without saying that these health problems have led to decreases in our overall life expectancy—never mind our number of healthy years. This will likely come as a shock to most readers, who have been spoon-fed nonsense about how our ancestors only expected to live for 40 years.

In reality, historical life expectancies are misleading because a relatively large percentage of children died before the age of five. This skewed life expectancy statistics downwards considerably. Also, many more men were expected to die in war, and women were expected to die in childbirth. Once these factors are accounted for, the average life expectancy has barely budged.

In fact, Paul Clayton and Judith Rowbotham found that the longest-lived and healthiest generation was born in the Victorian Age, specifically between the years 1850 and 1880. Men from these generations lived three years longer than we do today. Not only were they physically taller than subsequent generations, but they had greater muscle mass and less visceral fat. Interestingly, today's most common killers, being heart disease and cancer, were virtually unknown to the Victorian man.[94]

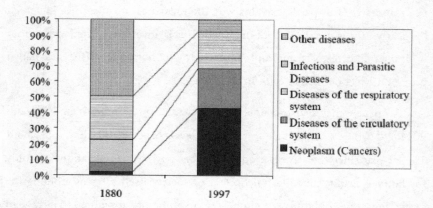

Clayton and Rowbotham note that the fountain of youth for the Victorians was their diet. Victorians ate traditional diets which were high in red meat—especially offal, organ meats—and animal fats. Vegetable fats and seed oils were not consumed because food chemists had not yet learned how to refine these inedible industrial lubricants into a food-adjacent product. Further, fruits and vegetables were significantly more nutritious.

There are two reasons for this. First, the switch to a plant-based diet has incentivized monoculture, which depletes soil of its micronutrients and trace minerals in a way that is simply not possible with grass-fed, pastured-raised cattle.

Second, modern crops are fertilized with potash. Potash primarily contains phosphorus, nitrogen, and potassium. Although these minerals greatly improve crop yields, they do not improve the nutritional profile of said crops. Instead, crops grow rapidly and deplete the soil of its trace minerals and micronutrients faster than nature can replenish them. This leads to crops devoid of nutrients, grown by plants which are relatively unhealthy—thereby requiring more pesticides and herbicides to protect them.

As a result, our modern diet is rich in calories yet largely devoid of nutrients. For example, research has shown that modern apples contain 50% less calcium, 85% less phosphorus, and 96% less iron than an apple of equivalent size from 1914.

On top of that, trace minerals such as boron and selenium are almost non-existent in modern produce.[95] This is a massive problem, because the human body—in particular the immune system—needs trace minerals in order to function. The lack of these trace minerals is contributing to America's overall health decline.

Although this is a complicated problem, there is a simple solution: make Americans rich again. The American diet shifted when American families could no longer afford to eat as well as their ancestors. Even today, the diets of upper middle-class Americans are far healthier than those of working-class Americans—steak is healthier than canned spam. As such, we have good reason to assume that Americans will choose steak and butter over cold cuts and rapeseed oil, if only they could afford it.

PART III

ARISTOTELIAN ECONOMICS, OR HOW TARIFFS WILL SAVE AMERICA

The British philosopher and mathematician Alfred North Whitehead commented "the safest general characterization of the European philosophical tradition is that it consists of a series of footnotes to Plato." This observation is basically true. Plato is emblematic of one of mankind's two main ways of conceptualizing the universe. Aristotle, Plato's greatest student, is the poster child of the other.

Plato believed that true knowledge could only be acquired through the application of deductive logic, not through sensory experience. As such, Plato viewed knowledge of theoretical concepts—he called these *forms*—as more valuable than real world examples of these concepts. For example, if one wants to understand *Justice* then he should begin with a general statement of what justice is, and then deduce how justice should be allied in specific cases. The philosopher is like a sculptor, who begins with a wire frame and then adds clay to produce a sculpture.

Modern economics is strongly influenced by Platonic philosophy. For example, when economists are confronted with a problem—the price of uranium is skyrocketing—they seek answers in economic theories. They will argue that the price *must* be skyrocketing because there is a shortage, or Russia is building more nuclear bombs etc. Economic theories provide answers. Likewise, Platonists believe that they can improve the economy by making it function more like the ideal theoretical economy.

Aristotle, on the other hand, believed that knowledge was acquired primarily through inductive logic. That is, the philosopher begins by observing many examples of his subject matter, and then uses logic to parse away that which is unimportant. For example, if one wants to understand Justice then he should go to the courthouse and watch its practical application. Once he has seen enough examples, he will be able to derive a rule. In his case, the philosopher is like a carver, who begins with a mountain and chips away at the rock until he reveals his statue.

In Part III of this book, we will explore economics from an Aristotelian perspective. We will do this by always paying attention to the actual data, and by relying upon historical examples be our guide. In Chapter 7, I will explain why economic doctrines—in particular the theory of comparative advantage that underpins free trade—often do not work in practice. In Chapter 8, I will answer the burning question: how do economies grow? In Chapter 9, we will conclude with a discussion of how tariffs can fix America's economy.

CHAPTER 7

AGAINST FREE TRADE

In 2018 I published a piece in the *Journal of American Greatness* defending President Donald Trump's tariff policy and criticizing global free trade. Mainstream "conservatives" were quick to distance themselves from my *heretical* views. After all, Republicans stand for freedom, liberty, and the right of the Communist Party of China to huck their slave-made wares in every Walmart in America—from sea to shining sea.

Ben Shapiro, who was at the time the Editor-in-Chief of the *Daily Wire*, went so far as to write a vitriolic response entitled "Yes, Tariffs are Still Stupid. Here's Why" in which he "debunked" my arguments. First and foremost, Shapiro was quick to remind his readers that "the reality is that [his] arguments on free trade have been supported by every major free market economist in history."[96]

Ben Shapiro was right. Every major "free market" economist supports free trade. Consider that in 1993, 283 experts—including twelve Nobel Prize winners, and famous "pop" economists like Milton Friedman and James Tobin—penned an open letter to the American people in defense of NAFTA.[97]

That said, I will remind you that just as every "free market" economist supports free trade, so too does every "Marxist economist" support socialism. Does the fact that Marxist economists support socialism prove that socialism works? No. The same is true of free market economists. Their opinions are logically irrelevant.

Ben Shapiro was engaging in sophistry—the art of persuading without evidence. More specifically, Shapiro employed the *Call to Authority* fallacy. This is a false argument that "proves" a point by referencing expert opinion. Although expert opinions may be rhetorically persuasive, they *prove* nothing. Why does 2 + 2 = 4? Because your kindergarten teacher said so? Of course not. Logical proof and empirical evidence exist independently of expert opinions, and must be evaluated independently.

Experts claim that free trade benefits America—and because the trade deficit is the result of freer global trade—the trade deficit itself must be good. This is false. We cannot trust experts simply because they have degrees, or because they are famous, or even because they won a Nobel Prize. Instead, we must evaluate their claims based on the evidence.

In Part I of this book, we surveyed America's economic destruction. Millions of Americans are chronically unemployed, and those who are lucky enough to have jobs have not had a pay raise since 1973. Meanwhile, America's industry has been hollowed out, and the economic dislocation has frayed the very fabric of society. In Part 2 we discovered that the trade deficit, an inevitable result of the offshoring vicious cycle, is the root cause of America's economic problems. The data clearly and unambiguously *proves* the experts wrong. Free trade did not work.

When confronted by this data, many economists shrug and say something along the lines of: "Free trade did not work in practice because it was not *real* free trade. Free trade works in theory, but we implemented it wrong." This deflection is wrong two reasons.

First, *real* free trade—much like *real* communism—is impossible. Different countries have different levels of economic development, legal systems, tax structures, histories, geographies, languages, cultures, and populations, all of which create market asymmetries between nations which are simply not present domestically.

At best, free traders can reduce tariffs and other *invisible* trade barriers, like transportation costs and legal disharmonies. America has done just that. Consider that America's average tariff rates dropped from well over 30% in the 1800s to effectively nil today. Further, *invisible* barriers to trade which were present in the 1800s, like the enormous cost of transporting bulk goods overseas, have been largely eradicated by technology. America trades more freely today than at any point in history, and our economy is worse than at any point in history. This is not a coincidence.

Second, global free trade does *not* work in theory. In this Chapter we will cover a lot of ground. We will begin by outlining some major epistemological problems with the "science" of liberal economics. The temple of economics is built on a shaky foundation, and we have good reasons to be skeptical of what the "experts" say.

Next, I will explain theory of *comparative advantage*, which is the economic logic which justifies global free trade, and show that it is *domain specific*. In other words, comparative advantage only works in certain circumstances, and it has been inappropriately used to justify global free trade. Finally, I will show that reality is more complicated than economic models, and therefore we should be careful we do not lock ourselves in the ivory tower.

KILLING HOMO ECONOMICUS

Even so every good tree bringeth forth good
fruit; but a corrupt tree bringeth forth evil fruit.
~ Jesus Christ

The science of economics is based on several false presumptions. Therefore, we must be skeptical of any conclusion derived from these presumptions—this includes the theory of free trade. The first false presumption is the myth of the *rational consumer*.

Economists assume that consumers make rational economic choices: they weigh the relative price and utility of products, and always buy the product which maximizes their relative wellbeing. For example, consumers prefer cheaper lollipops, provided they are of equal quality. The problem is that consumers are not rational—neither individually nor in aggregate. As a result, logical deductions made from this presumption will necessarily be suspect.

Daniel Kahneman, who won the Nobel Prize in economics for his work in establishing the field of *behavioral economics*, which views economics through the lens of psychology, has demonstrated that individual consumers do not always behave rationally. Instead, Kahneman found that humans make decisions based on two competing psychological "systems", which he explains in his book *Thinking Fast and Slow*.

System 1 operates subconsciously, automatically, and instantly, and makes decisions based on prior experience. For example, System 1 localizes the source of specific sounds in the environment and solves math equations like "2 + 2 = ?". *System 2*, is conscious, deliberate, and relatively slow reasoning. For example, you are likely using System 2 to understand the differences between the two systems right now. Importantly, economists assume that consumers *always* base their choices on System 2. This is untrue.

Human decisions are typically made by System 1, and those decisions which are made by System 2 are often colored by the psychological heuristics and biases present in System 1. For example, Kahneman ran an experiment where participates were shown either a big or a small number. A few minutes later, the participants were asked to determine reasonable prices for products. What Kahneman found is that participants who were psychologically *primed*, shown, the larger numbers were willing to pay more for products, and vice versa. This is irrational, as the numbers were completely unrelated.

Kahneman surmised that this was because System 1 interprets numbers according to the *anchoring and adjustment heuristic*. Essentially, the brain *anchors* to the last number with which it was primed, and then *adjusts* up or down from this number. Kahneman found many other heuristics and biases, mental shortcuts, used by System 1. These heuristics and biases are inherent in humanity, and therefore *guarantee* that individual consumers are *irrational*. As such, how can we trust the theory of free trade, when it is based on consumers behaving rationally? Would you trust a doctor who believes disease is caused by bad smells? Presumptions matter.

At this point, economists will admit that while individual consumers are not rational, they behave rationally in the aggregate, since individual biases and predilections are ironed-out by the group. In other words, the group balances out the individuals. This is untrue for two reasons. First, given that all individuals are irrational in the same ways—System 1 is uniformly irrational across humanity—then this irrationality will necessarily manifest in the aggregate, because there is no counterbalance. Second, groups themselves are subject to their own irrational dynamics.

In 1982 the French mathematician Benoit Mandelbrot published his landmark book *The Fractal Geometry of Nature*, in which he brought his pioneering work in the fields of fractal geometry and mathematics into the public consciousness. Essentially, Mandelbrot found that natural forms are often made of repeating patterns, which look similar at different levels of magnification. For example, a storm cloud is basically a large puff of cloud, and each puff is itself made up of smaller puffs of cloud. Extrapolating Mandelbrot's thesis provides a relevant critique of economics.

Economic organization is fractal. Therefore, we must expect that if irrationality is found at one level, it will be found at all levels. For example, a traditional family consists of a husband, wife, and children. The husband made big economic decisions for the family and the wife made day-to-day decisions. Today, many young people live alone, and make their own buying decisions. In all cases, those decision are not always rational.

So too, a corporation operates similarly to a traditional household: a CEO makes the most consequential economic decisions which bind the entire corporation, and those decisions are not always rational. For example, Kathleen Kennedy's insistence on promoting radical left-wing gender and racial ideology in Star Wars has cost Disney many hundreds of millions in lost box office revenue—and yet Disney's quest to play politics continues. This is not economically rational.

This sort of irrationality also occurs at the state level: governors and presidents make the most consequential economic decisions, and these decisions bind entire countries. For example, Stalin's collectivization of the USSR's farms caused widespread famine, killing millions of people and destroying the economic output of the Ukraine. This was certainly not economically rational.

Economics assumes that the market is a collection of millions of individuals making individual decisions, and any irrational decisions are smoothed out by the group. This is not necessarily true, since consequential economic decisions at different levels of organization are made by *individuals* at those respective levels of organization—we rarely have the large aggregates that economics presupposes.

Further, decisions at higher levels of organization are orders of magnitude more important than decisions at lowers levels, and often make the decisions for lower levels. Simply put, there is often no aggregate market mitigating or eliminating irrationality. Instead, we have a relatively small number of people making consequential economic decisions—especially regarding the question of global free trade—and these people do not act rationally.

Lastly, groups of people do not behave rationally because they have *emergent properties*. Emergent properties refer to dynamics, rules, or structures which do not exist until a certain scale is reached. These emergent properties may take on characteristics which are very different from the characteristics of their individual components.

For example, in 2021 a group of "investors" started buying stock in GameStop, both to prop-up a company which gave them fond childhood memories, and to stick it to investors on Wall Street, who were short-selling the stock. As a result, Stock in GameStop exploded from roughly $3.00 to over $80.00 in the space of a few weeks.

Investing in GameStop was irrational from an individual's economic perspective, but it made sense when looking at the group dynamics. Further, the "mob" which had coalesced was governed by emotion and spite—irrational qualities that should be *impossible* in a group dynamic, according to economists.

At the time of writing, GameStop is still trading at over $30.00 per share. This is not based on any improvement in the company's fundamentals, but because the mob is punishing Wall Street short sellers, and other investors are speculating that the stock may remain profitable due to volatility. The example of GameStop shows that groups are governed by their own dynamics, and that these dynamics are not always rational.

Classical economics is based on the presumption that consumers behave rationally. This is not true. Individual consumers do not necessarily behave rationally. Likewise, groups do not behave rationally—in fact, any student of history will note that the mob is often far more irrational than any individual in the mob. As such, we must be skeptical of economic theories which are ultimately derived from the myth of the rational consumer. The theory of free trade is no exception.

MISTAKING WASHING MACHINES FOR HURRICANES

The second false presumption undermining classical economics is that the economy is a *simple system*. In reality, the economy is a *complex system*. A simple system is a mode of order wherein cause and effect are related in a linear, one-to-one, way. That is, if you know the starting position of each systemic element, and you know what causes applied to said system, then it is possible to predict—with certainty—the outcome.

A classic example of a simple system is a billiards table. There is a one-to-one relationship between the *cause*, the direction and speed of the cueball, and the *effect*, the direct and speed of the 8-ball. Because of this, it is possible for the skilled player to *know* the outcome of a shot before he takes it. The same is true for most artificial modes of order, be it the game of chess or the operation of a washing machine.

On the other hand, a complex system is a mode of order in which cause and effect are related in a non-linear way. That is, a single cause may have multiple effects on the system, and these effects may themselves interact with each other in novel ways. Complex systems are subject to feedback loops, and may manifest emergent properties at different scales. As such, knowing the starting position of each systemic element, and the forces applied to said system, will not allow you to predict the outcome with any certainty.

That said, it is possible to forecast the probability of various end states. A classic example of a complex system is the weather. There is a non-linear relationship between the various inputs, such as level of solar activity, humidity, wind speed, and the end result—which is a 30% chance of blue skies and a 70% chance of thunderstorms. It is not possible to know *a priori* what the weather will look like next week. At best, meteorologists and make and continuously-update forecasts based on the best-available data. The same is true for many organic and natural systems, be it human history or a hurricane.

The economy is a complex system. In fact, it is one of the most complex systems known to man. Consider that the causes of weather patterns are the interplay of solar radiation and water droplets. These causes are simple causes which, when isolated, operate in a linear way. These interactions are complicated, but not nearly as complicated as those in the economy.

The economy is the manifestation of countless individual choices. Often, choice is the product of System 1. However, choices made in accordance with System 2 are the result of the deliberate exercise of free will, and are an expression of human consciousness. Philosophers disagree as to whether consciousness originates with God or is an emergent property of the human brain, but all agree that the mind is perhaps the *most* complex organic system.

When this fact is combined with the fractal nature of economic organization—different layers make different decisions that have ripple effects between the layers—it becomes obvious that the economy is the king of complex systems. Further, the economy is subject to many complex feedback loops, like the off-shoring vicious cycle, which can turn predictions on their head.

Economists are guilty of treating the economy like a simple system by acquiring "knowledge" as follows. First, economists observe the economy. Second, they notice patterns. Third, they formulate rules from these patterns. Fourth, economists combine rules into theories and models. Fifth, theories and models are used to make predictions.

In this way, economists tell us now only how the economy works, but how it *will* work in the future. As we have seen, prediction is simply not possible when dealing with a complex system. As a result, predictions made from these models—like free trade will create jobs and raise wages—are often completely wrong.

That said, it is possible to understand and learn from a complex system like the economy—it just requires a different methodology. Economists are right to begin by observing and noticing patterns. However, economists should be loath to develop rules from these patterns. Even a rule as basic as "demand decreases as price increases" has numerous exceptions, such as in the market for luxury goods. Likewise, individual motivations—like spite in the case of GameStop—routinely cause this rule to be violated in all sorts of unpredictable contexts. As such, economic events and processes should be studied on their own terms in the same way that historians study historical events.

Good historians seek to understand past events based on the evidence. Specific events are explained in specific terms, rather than as the inevitable results of a historical rule. In this way, we understand how and why history unfolded. Importantly, historians do not attempt to create theories or models from which they claim to predict the future. Instead, history is valuable because it provides us with examples of what could happen—and given a large enough sample size, we can even determine tentative likelihoods of different outcomes. For example, 200 years of history shows us that America prospered with high tariffs, despite the economic rules to the contrary.

As Mark Twain famously surmised: "history does not repeat itself, but it often rhymes." The same is true of economics. Until economists approach the discipline as an art, rather than a science, they will continue to do more harm than good—both to society and to their own credibility.

"BORNE AWAY... AND LOST IN DARKNESS AND DISTANCE"

In Mary Shelley's *Frankenstein*, the doctor reanimates dead flesh through alchemy and electricity—and sheer human will. Upon seeing his abomination come to life, Dr. Frankenstein flees his laboratory. The monster survives, and seeks revenge on his maker by hurting that which he loves. This gothic tragedy shows how our creations take on their own lives and may behave contrary to our intentions. The same is true of the theory of *comparative advantage*, which is the theoretical linchpin for global free trade. The next few sections of this chapter will detail why comparative advantage simply does not work.

David Ricardo (d.1823) explains comparative advantage in his treatise *On the Principles of Political Economy and Taxation*. At its heart, the theory is straightforward: countries should trade things they are relatively good at making for things they are relatively bad at making. This makes the economy more efficient, and therefore makes everyone richer, since more stuff is made with less overall work.

To illustrate his point, Ricardo came up with a now-classic example. It goes like this: suppose there are two countries, England and Portugal. Both make cloth and wine. Now pretend it takes England 100 man-hours to make a bolt of cloth, and 120 hours to make a barrel of wine. As such, it takes 220 hours to make one unit of each. In this case, England is relatively better at making cloth than wine.

Now suppose in Portugal it takes only 90 hours to make a bolt of cloth, and 80 hours to make the wine, that is, 170 hours to make one unit of each. Notice how that Portugal is *absolutely* better at making *both* cloth *and* wine, since it takes the Portuguese less time to make either commodity. However, Portugal is *relatively* better at making wine than cloth. Therefore, it can be said that, relative to England, Portugal has a *comparative advantage* in making wine, and that

England has one in making cloth—each country is better at making one thing than in making the other, and it makes logical sense for them to specialize in making only the thing they each make best, England makes cloth and Portugal makes wine. Then, they can trade with each other to acquire the other product.

Logically and mathematically, comparative advantage makes sense. If neither country specialized, it would take 220 hours for England to make one unit of cloth and one unit of wine, while Portugal would take 170 hours. However, if they both specialized and traded, then the same labor could make 2.2 units of cloth and 2.125 units of wine—like magic, specialization and trade makes everyone richer.

When applying comparative advantage globally, it follows that if every region specialized in making goods for which it has a comparative advantage, then the global economy would be maximally efficient, and therefore the world would be richer. The problem is that the theory of comparative advantage has limitations that economists typically ignore.

The most powerful critique of comparative advantage comes from David Ricardo himself. In his book, he acknowledges that his theory is *domain*-specific, meaning that it only applies when certain conditions are met. In a way, the theory of comparative advantage contains the seeds of its own destruction. Ricardo writes:

> ...*it would undoubtedly be advantageous to the capitalists [and consumers] of England... [that] the wine and cloth should both be made in Portugal [and that] the capital and labour of England employed in making cloth should be removed to Portugal for that purpose.*

Ricardo explicitly states that, according to his theory, it makes sense for England to import both cloth and wine from Portugal, since Portugal can make them more efficiently, and that England's cloth-making industry should be *offshored* to Portugal. This would result in offshoring and trade deficits—exactly what has happened in real life whenever America signs a trade deal with a developing nation.

Of course, Ricardo is not a stupid man, and he knows full well this would be a losing strategy for England—if England imported everything and made nothing, it would have no economy. Furthermore, England would be vulnerable to foreign suppliers, just as the United States depends upon Saudi Arabia and other fair-weather friends and sometimes hostile nations for its oil.

Ricardo adds an intellectual buttress to ensure that the temple of trade will not collapse: he writes "most men of property [will be] satisfied with a low rate of profits in their own country, rather than seek[ing] a more advantageous employment for their wealth in foreign nations." There you have it, Ricardo's argument—the entire theory of comparative advantage, global free trade itself—is premised on the assumption that most people love their country more than money, and will invest domestically out of the goodness of their hearts.

Unfortunately, Gordon Gekko was right: "greed is good" is the name of their game.

Ricardo also used a more technical defense of comparative advantage from this obvious flaw. He argued that offshoring is impossible because *capital is* immobile—that is, England's textile mills *could not* be moved to Portugal anyway. This is the condition that I mentioned before—comparative advantage is domain-specific because it only applies when capital is stuck and offshoring cannot occur, such as when trade happens within a nation, or when something prevents commerce from relocating.

To be fair, when Ricardo wrote his *Principles*, capital was indeed largely immobile. His theory of comparative advantage worked because, in the early 19th century, transportation was an order of magnitude more expensive, machinery could not legally be exported from Britain, tariffs on manufactured goods exceeded 50%, capital markets were undeveloped in most countries, and endemic warfare prevented a large-scale commodity trade. Therefore, this hypothetical problem remained purely hypothetical for Ricardo. This is no longer true.

Capital is highly mobile in today's economy. A factory can be relocated from the United States to China in short order, and transportation for bulk goods is incredibly (almost unbelievably) cheap. In fact, in the decades after Ricardo's death in 1823, capital grew ever more mobile, and his hypothetical dilemma soon became real.

Throughout the 1800s there was a steady increase of capital outflows from Great Britain, as British investors built projects abroad seeking higher return. In 1815, £10 million was invested abroad. In 1825, this climbed to £100 million, and by 1870 it was £700 million. By 1914 (the peak) over 35 percent of Britain's national wealth was held abroad—Britain suffered a severe, decades long shortfall in domestic investment.[98] Likewise, economic and industrial growth slowed to a crawl, as the British market was flooded with German and American products. As we saw in Part I, this is exactly what is happening to America today.

Perhaps the best way to end this article is to compare what happened to Ricardo's hypothetical England and Portugal with what happened in the real countries. In his example, Portugal gets rich by maximizing its comparative advantage in wine, while England gets rich by doing so with cloth. Both countries trade, both benefit. Reality is harsh.

In 1703, the two countries signed the Treaty of Methuen, which, among other things, exempted English cloth from a Portuguese import-prohibition. In the following decades, cheap English imports destroyed Portugal's textile industry, and Portugal indeed resorted to exporting wine. Soon afterward, England gained a textile monopoly in Portugal, which allowed Britain to drive up prices above-market, expand her increasingly-advanced textile industry— this stimulated the mechanical and engineering breakthroughs that birthed the

Industrial Revolution—and buy up Portugal's vineyards, thereby securing both industries. As it turns out not all industries are of equal value—cloth was more lucrative than wine. In the end, the Treaty of Methuen deal helped England industrialize and grow rich—at Portugal's expense.

These two basic truths—*people are greedy* and *capital is mobile*—completely destroy comparative advantage by invalidating its underlying premise, and relegate it to the intellectual curiosity shop of history. Ricardo was a smart man who recognized his theory's limits, and it is too bad his ideas have been bastardized to justify global free trade in a world where his theory was never meant to apply. May Ricardo's monster rest in peace.

A NEW WITTENBERG

In addition to the critique of comparative advantage provided by David Ricardo himself, we will explore five additional critiques. First, the theory of comparative advantage offers no predictive power. If we apply the theory of comparative advantage worldwide, the globe looks like a spider web of interconnecting trade routes, linking everywhere to everywhere else; each place specializes as much as possible to maximize its comparative advantage in a given type of output.

For example, America has a massive comparative advantage in growing corn, while China has a massive comparative advantage in making Polly Pocket toys. According to the theory, not only should each country specialize its production—no matter how low the output is on the value-added chain—but it postulates that there should be a correlation between the wealth of the country and the degree of its specialization. That is, the more specialized, the more of its comparative advantage it is likely leveraging, the richer it should be. This is complete nonsense.

Richer countries usually produce more advanced output. In fact, there is a very strong, and proven, statistical correlation between the wealth of a country and the complexity of its exports.[99] Thus, it is a safe bet to assume a country exporting jet engines and semiconductors is richer than one exporting jerked beef and cornmeal. There are exceptions, like the Gulf States, but these exceptions prove the rule.

Reality shows us that richer countries have more diverse economies. This is because industries tend to cluster, forming self-fueling industrial ecosystems. There is a reason that the term *banana republic* is synonymous with poverty.[vii] Comparative advantage predicts that specialization in an output, regardless of its complexity, makes countries rich. This is false. Rich countries have diverse economies that make sophisticated things. If the theory predicts a conclusion, but the opposite is true, then the theory is wrong. Therefore, comparative advantage is wrong. It is that simple.

Second, comparative advantage is domain specific in that it only applies in situations where nations trade for goods. It does not apply when nations sell assets or promise debt in exchange for goods. Remember, comparative advantage states that countries will produce more total goods if they specialize their production and trade for the remaining goods. However, if a country is able to sell or promise in exchange for goods, there is a possibility that they will manufacture *no* goods. This unequivocally reduces the total goods created, and instead simply redistributes existing wealth.

For example, if England exchanged old curtains from their manor houses, as opposed to newly-made cloth, to Portugal for wine, it is possible that current production could decrease, as long as there are still old curtains to trade. In this instance, wealth is simply shuffled around rather than created. Current output actually *decreases*, because instead of making trade goods, England trades stuff that was made in the past. The same logic applies to debt. This process is

---

vii The term "banana republic" was coined to describe the US dependencies in Central America whose economic vitality was predicated upon the export of a single product: bananas. It has since taken on a disparaging connotation due to CIA involvement in the region, however the economic truth behind it today has lost none of its potency: a country that exports a single product is going to be a basket case. See: Fletcher & Reinert (93).

unsustainable: at some point England will run out of assets and debts, and will need to either decrease their consumption of wine or increase their production of cloth. There is no such thing as a free lunch.

Third, comparative advantage only works in a sterile platonic economy. The real world is better understood in terms of *competitive advantage*, which considers not just raw efficiency, but a host of contributing factors that give industries or countries a competitive edge.[100] Because of this, global free trade has led to highly efficient American factories being replaced by less efficient, but nominally cheaper, Chinese factories. This often results in a patently less efficient allocation of resources.[101]

Fourth, *factors of production*, like buildings, machines, and people do not always move seamlessly between industries. Let me explain. Pretend America signs a new trade deal with Nepal. As it turns out, the Nepalese are very skilled at building dirt-cheap jet turbines. In exchange, the Nepalese buy excessive amounts of sirloin steaks. This situation is bad for American turbine manufacturers, who either close or relocate to Nepal, and good for American ranchers.

The problem is that all of those US jet turbine factories, the machinery, and the technicians are now unproductive, since the capital used in turbine building cannot be used in the ranching industry—ranches do not need the factories, nor do engineers make good cowboys. The factories and machines will need to be repurposed or scrapped, and the workers will need to find other employment, which as we have seen, usually pays less. Repurposing and retraining takes time, and sometimes the capital sits idly for years, if not decades.

For example, many factories in the Rustbelt were abandoned and have remained dilapidated since the 1990s. The disparity between what the economy could produce at full output, if capital was used rather than mothballed or transitioned, and what the economy is producing is called the *Okun Gap*. When this is accounted for, the benefits of free trade are much smaller than our politicians and economists lead us to believe.

Fifth, maximizing comparative advantage does not cause long run economic growth, because long run economic growth is tied to technological improvements. Chapter 8 of this book is wholly dedicated to this issue, and therefore I am simply adumbrating the critique here for posterity.

A LAWYER AND A SECRETARY WALK INTO A BAR...

Milton Friedman is one of America's most famous "pop" economists. In addition to winning a Nobel Prize, Friedman has been instrumental in popularizing teachings from the Chicago School of economics. In his manifesto *Free to Choose*, he explains to the American public why free trade *always* benefits the economy.

Friedman begins his "economic case for free trade" by arguing that free trade enables America to buy cheaper goods. These cheap imports benefit American consumers more than they hurt American producers. To begin with, this is objectively untrue. As we saw in Part I of this book, the economic data clearly shows that America's economy has been hollowed out during the free trade period. Millions are unemployed, wages have stagnated, and the quality of goods has decreased. In Part II, we saw how the trade deficit and the offshoring vicious cycle sufficiently account for this economic deterioration.

Not only does the economic data prove Friedman wrong, he is also wrong theoretically. Friedman fails to mention that every American consumer is also a producer—people work for the money they spend. As such, what hurts producers inevitably hurts consumers. If an industry is offshored, its former workers must find work in another industry. As we saw, this decreases wages for all consumers. Over time, the "cheap" goods are no longer cheap.

Further, because America exports capital-intensive goods, like aircraft and software, and imports labor-intensive goods, like dress shirts and apples, trade destroys more jobs than it creates. While this may increase economic efficiency, it impoverishes many more consumers than it enriches. Because of the asymmetry between America's imports and exports, free trade with the Third World would still hurt American workers even if there was no trade deficit.

Continuing along this vein, Friedman simplistically claims that imports are good because they are our "benefit" from trade. He states that Americans gain from importing as much as possible, while exporting as little as possible. Essentially, a trade deficit means that we get more for less. Friedman goes so far as to say that when managing your household "you would surely prefer to pay less for more rather than the other way around, yet that would be termed an "unfavorable balance of payments" [or deficit] in foreign trade." This statement is, frankly, idiotic.

To be clear, running a trade deficit does not mean we receive more for less. We pay for the goods by selling our assets and promising our debt. This would be akin to a household pawning grandmother's wedding ring and maxing-out the credit cards to pay for groceries. No prudent person runs their household this way. Neither is it prudent for us to run our nation this way.

Friedman also claims it is "simply not true that high-wage American workers are... threatened by "unfair" competition from low-wage foreign workers" because currency markets always balance out, and because Americans benefit from cheaper imports.[102] This is incorrect.

As we have seen, American runs massive trade deficits in advanced technology products, and is suffering from brain-drain to places like China and India. As more American companies offshore their research and development, America will continue to publish proportionally less papers and register fewer patents. This directly threatens high wage American workers, and America's long term economic prospects, contrary to Friedman's assertions.

Not only that, but Friedman's assumption that we should only care about "high-wage' workers is *evil*. The American Dream is for everyone. By offshoring low, middle, and increasingly high-paying jobs, we cut the ladder out from under those who are trying to climb it.

Americans are finding it harder and harder to get the skills they need because we are offshoring our "steppingstone" jobs. Also, remember that most Americans are not wealthy. Most Americans work for a living at a normal job. Our economic policy should work for everyone—not just Milton Friedman's billionaire friends.

Finally, we will address Friedman's most famous analogy explaining the logic of comparative advantage. Friedman asks us to consider the following example: a lawyer is twice as good at typing as his paralegal, but he is five-times as good a lawyer. Because of his comparative advantage, it makes sense for him to pay the secretary to do his typing, even though he is better in absolute terms, so that he can maximize his income as a lawyer. This makes sense, but only if you are the lawyer.

The best long-term strategy for the secretary is to go back to school and become a lawyer too. Even if the former secretary makes less than the first lawyer, she will still make far more than she did as a secretary. This is because it is better to be bad at something good than be good at something bad—ever notice how even bad investment bankers make more than the best busboys?

The obvious defense of this critique is to say that America is the lawyer, not the secretary. To this I have two responses. First, in the example it is in the lawyer's best interest that his secretary remains a secretary, since if she became a lawyer, she would compete with him, and he would either need to hire another secretary or do his own typing.

If this is a valid analogy—and the Nobel Prize-winning Milton Friedman believes it is—then it follows that it is in America's interests to prevent other countries from advancing to the point that they compete with us. In other words, we should refrain from investing abroad, and we should avoid buying advanced technology products from our competitors. This implication is precisely the opposite of what Friedman recommends.

TIRRA LIRRA, TIRRA LIRRA.

In his poem 'The Lady of Shalott' Lord Tennyson tells us how a beautiful princess is locked in a tower. She sees the outside world through a mirror. One sunlit day she sees the reflection of Sir Lancelot flash into the mirror. Infatuated, she escapes her tower and rows a boat to Camelot. But a curse comes upon her, and she dies before she reaches Lancelot.

Like the Lady of Shalott, ideologues like Ben Shapiro or Milton Friedman sit in an ivory tower and view the economy through their magic mirrors. In the end, they mistake the mirror for reality, and defend free trade in light of the reflected images. Of course, reflections are not reality, and economic theory is not the economy. Free trade does not work in practice because America's competitors do not play by the same rules.

To begin with, China systematically violates a multitude of General Agreement on Tariffs and Trade ("GATT") and World Trade Organization ("WTO") agreements by creating and maintaining entry barriers to the Chinese market. In other words, China is largely free to sell their products in America, but America is not free to sell products in China.

These flagrant violations of international law include legal barriers to imports, like absurd or incomprehensible regulations; dumping goods in foreign markets, that is selling large quantities of a product below cost so as to drive out local competition, and then raising prices after they have a monopoly; and suppressing labor rights for Chinese workers, which lowers labor costs by an estimated 47-86%, depending upon the industry.[103]

China also provides extensive subsidies for their exporters. Between 2000 and 2006, roughly 33% of Chinese exporters sold over 90% of their goods abroad. For context, only 0.7% of American exporters did the same. [104] Additionally, exporters are rewarded with preferential land-use policies, easier access to finance, or exemptions from various industrial or commercial taxes, which is in direct contravention or WTO rules. [105]

This highlights just how dedicated the Chinese are to preying upon Western markets. China does not play fair: Chinese companies are free to compete in America, but American companies cannot compete in China.

Researchers in fields as diverse as political science, economics, evolutionary biology, pathology, botany, zoology, psychology, philosophy, and various branches of mathematics have studied the optimal levels of cooperation between *groups*. Groups have been variously defined as different species of creatures, genetically-related plants and animals, corporations, and nations. In all cases, researchers have converged on the same finding: in-group cooperation, combined with out-group indifference, is the optimal survival strategy.

This is because groups which only share resources within their in-group, *ethnocentrism*, boost their group's changes of survival. In turn, this boosts their chance of survival. Meanwhile, groups which share resources indiscriminately with all groups, *humanitarianism*, increase both their chances of survival and their competitor's chance of survival. As a result, ethnocentric groups always outcompete humanitarian groups in the long run.

A study from McGill University ran simulations which modeled in-group competition using different cooperative strategies. [106] They found that in the early stages, where competition was relatively low and resources plentiful, ethnocentrism and humanitarian cooperative strategies were equally successful. However, in the long run ethnocentric cooperation outcompeted all other rivals.

Again, this is because in-group cooperation limits benefits towards an individual's particular group, whether it be his family, corporation, or nation. By embracing free trade, America has placed itself squarely in the humanitarian cooperative strategy—we trade with everyone even if they do not reciprocate. China, meanwhile, placed itself firmly in the ethnocentric cooperative strategy. They trade with us but only on asymmetric terms. In the long run, free trade— like all other humanitarian strategies—is a death sentence. It simply does not work in an environment where other nations can refuse to reciprocate.

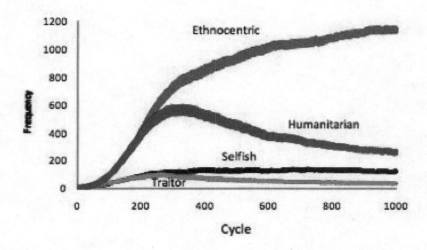

"Free trade" with China is anything but free. Trade with China is fundamentally asymmetrical—their policies are designed to prey upon America's apathy and weakness. By doing nothing, we pit American companies against Chinese companies, backed by the might of China's communist dictatorship.

That is not a free market, and it is not a fair fight. In the end, free trade theory fails because economics is not about "efficiency" or "profit" or any other buzzword. Economics is about power. Money is a means to an end. China understands this, and America must learn this lesson too before the magic mirror cracks and the arcane curse comes upon us.

CHAPTER 8

ON THE WEALTH OF NATIONS

Afraid his son would steal his throne, Dionysius I, Tyrant of Syracuse, locked the boy away in a tower. Never leaving his prison, the boy learned about the world from his teachers and books. War, rhetoric, politics—he mastered them all. The boy was Leonidas without a spear, Themistocles without silver, Pericles without his words.

Everything changed when Dionysius I died. The boy—now a man—ascended the throne. Yet for all his knowledge he lost battles, forgot speeches, and impoverished his people. Dionysius II even invited Plato to help him rule as a philosopher-king. But all Plato's wisdom proved worthless. Plato was lucky to escape Syracuse with his life. Although Dionysius II knew everything, he knew *nothing*. Logic is not experience. Knowledge is not skill. Theory is not reality. Dionysius never realized that his knowledge was ignorance, and his ignorance, knowledge. He died in disgrace in 344 B.C.

As we saw in Chapter 7, this lesson remains as true today as it did two millennia ago. Economic theories often do more harm than good. Nevertheless, this has not stopped centuries of historians, economists, and mathematicians from attempting to answer the most important question in economics: "how do countries get rich?" Unfortunately, all main lines of inquiry have been dead ends.

The reason for this is not because my predecessors were stupid, quite the contrary, their explanations failed because they mistook their logic for experience, knowledge for skill, and theory for reality. In a sense, economists have followed in the intellectual footsteps of Dionysius II. So too have their theories left their homeland in poverty and disgrace.

In this Chapter I intend to succeed where my predecessors failed, and will answer the question "how do countries get rich?" First, we will begin by exploring and evaluating the main competing theories. Specifically, we will look at the *classical* explanation as described by Adam Smith, then the *geographical* explanation popularized by Jared Diamond, followed by the *cultural* explanation epitomized by *Max Weber*, and finally *biological* explanation proffered by Richard Lynn. As we will see, all of these approaches are fundamentally incomplete. Second, I will explain that long run economic growth is simply a function of technological growth. Third, we will explore *how* to improve technology and grow the economy.

AGAINST THE WEALTH OF NATIONS

Adam Smith published his magnum opus *The Wealth of Nations* in 1776. Not only did Smith's work help cement economics as an independent academic discipline, but it was one of the first works to ask and answer the question: "how do countries get rich?" In a sense, all of economics—including this book—is a footnote to Adam Smith. Perhaps unsurprisingly, Adam Smith's answer to this question is on the right track, but simply does not go far enough.

Smith's contention is that economic growth is caused by increased productivity, that is, making more output in the same amount of time. Smith clarifies his logic with the following example: an artisan makes nails. Every day he rolls out his wire, snips it to the appropriate length, sharpens one end and flattens the other, and then packages them for sale. This highly skilled artisan can make 100 nails per day.

Now imagine that this artisan hired more workers. He divides the labor up so that each worker can focus on a particular task: one worker rolls the wire, another snips it, and so on. In this case, Smith notes that the shop could make 4,000 nails per day. Why? The division of labor means that each worker can focus on one task without interruption. This allows them to work significantly faster, and produce better quality products. Rather than being a jack of all trades, each worker becomes a master of one.

Essentially, increased productivity through the division of labor creates wealth. Therefore, policies which allow for further division of labor—such as free markets—will cause economic growth.

Smith also implies that *capital accumulation* causes economic growth. That is, the division of labor allows each worker to acquire more specialized tools and machinery to complete his task. The acquisition and deployment of this capital equipment is integral to countries becoming rich. For example, a country with more looms will invariably produce more cloth than a country which has not accumulated looms. For Smith, increasing productivity through the division of labor and accumulation of capital is the key to economic growth.

Smith is correct on both counts. The key to economic growth is to increase productivity. Further, capital accumulation is an important way to increase productivity. However, Smith's theory has limited explanatory power. At a certain point labor will be divided to maximum efficiency, and although one can always acquire further capital, there is a limit to how much can be deployed by one worker. When this point is reached, no further economic growth is possible in Smith's model. As such, the real engine of economic growth is *exogenous* to Smith's theory—it is unaccounted for.

Unfortunately, subsequent classical economists who have written on this subject have made the same mistake as Smith. They have either assumed that Smith's description of economic growth is complete, or they have implied that economic growth is an exogenous condition, and instead focused on raising productivity by other means. David Ricardo, for example, focused on increasing the division of labor through maximizing *comparative advantage*.

AGAINST GUNS, GERMS, AND STEEL

In 1748 Charles de Montesquieu wrote *De L'Espirit des Lois*. Montesquieu observed that countries located in temperate latitudes were typically richer than those located in tropical latitudes. As such, he hypothesized climate was an integral component in explaining the wealth of nations.

More recently, Jared Diamond has argued that the environment is not merely a contributing factor, it is the *only* factor which explains the long-term differences in national wealth. In his most famous work *Guns, Germs, and Steel*, Diamond writes:

> *The striking difference between the long-term histories of people of the different continents have been due not to innate differences in the peoples themselves but to differences in their environments.*[107]

Diamond's main line of argument is that Eurasia developed both economically and technologically, while Africa and the Americas stagnated, because of environmental differences between the continents. These are summarized as follows.

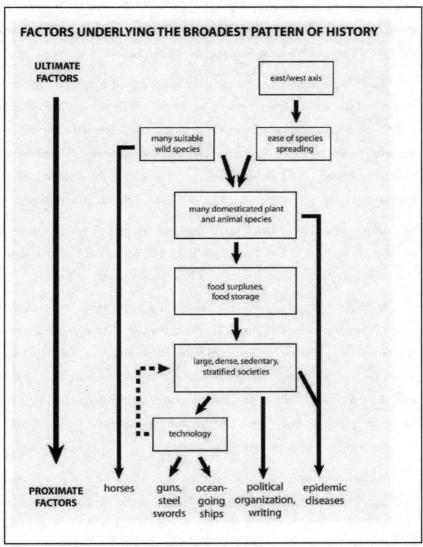

FACTORS UNDERLYING THE BROADEST PATTERN OF HISTORY

ULTIMATE FACTORS

east/west axis

many suitable wild species

ease of species spreading

many domesticated plant and animal species

food surpluses, food storage

large, dense, sedentary, stratified societies

technology

PROXIMATE FACTORS — horses — guns, steel swords — ocean-going ships — political organization, writing — epidemic diseases

Teacher Consultant Mike Fogel's Adaptation of Jared Diamond, *Guns, Germs, and Steel*

First, Diamond argues that Eurasia had more flora and fauna which could be domesticated, giving Eurasians the benefits of animal power and disease resistance. Meanwhile, the other continents lacked domesticable animals. Second,

Eurasia was traversable along the east-west axis, which lacked major barriers. This allowed the transmission of people, goods, and information between the continents. In contrast, Africa and the Americas are primarily oriented on a north-south axis, which made transportation difficult.

Third, Diamond claims that the diffusion of information into and out of Africa and the Americas was limited by the Sahara Desert and the Atlantic and Pacific oceans. Forth, Eurasia is the largest continent and therefore had the most people. While Diamond is correct that environmental factors have likely contributed to the differences in national wealth, these factors do not adequately explain why some modern countries are rich and others are poor.

Diamond's evidence can be easily dismissed. First, there are many animals and plants which could have been domesticated in Africa and the Americas— and some were in fact domesticated after European colonists arrived.

Second, Diamond's claim that Eurasia was more easily traversed than Africa or the Americas is incorrect. In reality, the Gobi Desert and Himalayan Mountains were just as formidable natural obstacles as the Sahara Desert, which could be easily circumvented by sailing down Africa's east coast. In any case, there was ample trade across the Sahara throughout the prehistorical and historical periods, and this is why Africans did not succumb to disease when Europeans arrived, as did the Amerindians.

Further, writing evolved independently in three locations in Eurasia, in Egypt, Mesopotamia, and China, implying that the level of informational cross-pollination assumed by Diamond simply did not exist. If it did, it is likely that writing would have evolved once and spread like wildfire.

Third, Diamond's claim that Eurasia's east-west orientation mattered is dubious. I say this because Africa has a very large east-west axis of approximately 4,000 miles, whereas Mesoamerica's east-west axis is just 500 miles, while the Peruvian east-west axis is just 300 miles. Nevertheless, America was home to the Maya, Olmecs, Toltecs, Aztecs, and Inca, whose civilizations were arguably more advanced than any comparative civilizations in sub-Saharan Africa.

Accordingly, we can deduce that the length of the east-west axis is not particularly relevant. Likewise, the three primary Eurasian civilizations based around the Mediterranean, Indian subcontinent, and China proper, were each approximately as wide as Africa, and were isolated to a similar degree—at least in the prehistorical period which Diamond believes is determinative.

Fourth, Diamond's environmental factors cannot explain contemporary differences between the wealth of nations. For example, his claim that modern Africa is poor today because of environmental "bad luck" 10,000 years ago is patently absurd. This not only ignores the vicissitudes in the wealth of Eurasian nations throughout history—after the fall of Rome large portions of Europe were reduced to abject poverty—but it does not explain why formerly poor Asian countries adopted European technology and organization, whereas African countries did not.

That said, environmental factors explain why some countries are rich. For example, Saudi Arabia is rich entirely because of its vast oil reserves. Nevertheless, environmental factors cannot explain why other countries which lack lucrative natural resources, like Germany or Great Britain, are rich. Further, having abundant resources does not cause economic growth, that is, why more resources are extracted or produced each year. As such, economic growth is also exogenous to the environmental explanation.

ON THE MYTH OF CULTURAL EXCEPTIONALISM

Many thinkers have claimed that some nations are rich, and other poor, because of cultural differences. Basically, some cultures are better at producing material wealth than others. This idea is ancient.

For example, Thucydides (d. 400 B.C.) writes in his History of the Peloponnesian War that what made Athens exceptional was its national spirit, its ingenuity, and its optimism. Likewise, Polybius (d. 118 B.C.) wrote in The Histories that Rome's power lay with its people's shrewd, prideful, and stubborn demeanor. More recently, the German sociologist Max Weber (d. 1920) hypothesized that the "protestant work ethic" was responsible for the wealth of Western Europe and its colonies, like the United States of America, as compared to the less dynamic economies of Catholic or Orthodox Europe.

Cultural explanations for economic growth are profoundly compelling—one can hardly read Thucydides and not be convinced that Athens was rich because the Athenian people were themselves exceptional. Likewise, one would be hard-pressed to explain the massive disparity in wealth between North and South Korea without referencing cultural and political differences. Culture matters. And yet, culture does not matter. Let me explain this paradox.

To begin with, it is obvious that certain cultural practices are better at fostering economic growth than others. For example, cultures that protect property rights provide strong incentives for people to create and accumulate material wealth—why would anyone sacrifice their life building a home or a business if it did not benefit themselves or their families? Conversely, cultures that eschew private property virtually guarantee that people will scrape by doing the bare minimum. Why work hard when you are paid the same as a slacker? In this way, cultural differences go a long way to explaining the economic disparities between North and South Korea, Botswana and Lesotho, and the U.S.A. and the U.S.S.R during the Cold War—despite these respective examples being relatively analogous according to other objective demographic or geographic standards.

Paradoxically, culture does not matter whatsoever. For example, most of us would agree that the U.S.S.R's culture was about as antithetical to economic growth as possible. On paper, people were not free to own private property, create or invest in their own businesses, or to speak or think freely. Compare this to Americans in the 1900s, who were perhaps the freest generations in human history. Early Americans enjoyed robust property rights, a strong and stable currency, and enjoyed an unabridged ability to speak their mind. Yet despite these enormous cultural differences between the U.S.S.R. and 1900's America, the U.S.S.R.'s economic output in 1970 was far and beyond America's during the 1970's—both in terms of raw economic output, and the value of this output.

This is because the U.S.S.R.'s economy had benefitted from a century of technological growth, which enabled its famously "unproductive" workers to produce more per capita than their historical American "competitors". To iron out any confusion on this point: consider again the two Koreas. In 2019 South Korea GDP at PPP was about $1.6 trillion. Meanwhile, North Korea's GDP at PPP was estimated at $72 billion. That is, South Korea's GDP is 11 times larger than North Korea's, after accounting for population differences. Culture matters. And yet, North Korea's 2019 GDP at PPP was roughly 18 times bigger than was South Korea's GDP in 1960, even after adjusting for inflation. Culture does not matter.

Technology, not culture, is the operative element in economic growth. At the end of the day, no amount of culturally-approved elbow grease will motivate a human to move more dirt with a shovel than with a bulldozer, to harvest more wheat with a scythe than a combine, or to transport more coal with a wheelbarrow than with a dump truck. Technology allows exponentially more to be done with less. Therefore, it is technology—not culture—that drives economic growth.

A NONLINEAR CRITIQUE OF BIOLOGICAL REDUCTIONISM

In the landmark book *IQ and the Wealth of Nations*, Richard Lynn and Tatu Vanhanen argue "intelligence of the populations has been a major factor responsible for the national differences in economic growth and for the gap in per capita income between rich and poor nations".[108]

Although their work has received harsh criticism from the political left—who accuse them of racism for the crime of *noticing* racial differences in IQ, a proxy for intelligence—Lynn and Vanhanen's thesis has merit. In fact, national IQ is a not an inconvenient reality, it is a *necessary* component of any serious answer to the fundamental economic question: what causes economic growth, and why are some countries rich and others poor?

Lynn and Vanhanen begin by defining *intelligence*. They note intelligence is essentially a person's efficiency at "problem solving, learning, remembering, and [performing tasks] ranging from complex mathematical to logical problems to simple reaction times involving the speed of pressing a button on a keyboard when a light comes on."[109]

Further, intelligence can be summarized in the *intelligence quotient* ("IQ"), because all types of intelligence which can be tested are correlated with one another. That is, someone who is good at solving math puzzles will probably be good at word games, and he will likely have fast reaction times.

The opposite is also true. Frankly, this fact should be obvious to anyone who has interacted with other people in any context: smart people tend to be relatively good at everything, whereas dumb people tend to be relatively bad at everything. Knowledge is domain specific. Intelligence is fairly general.

Unsurprisingly, Lynn and Vanhanen found strong correlations between individual earnings and IQ. That is, smarter people earned more money. Anecdotally this makes sense: in our daily lives we typically find that our smarter family members typically run successful businesses, or are professionals like doctors or lawyers.

Conversely, our dumbest high school classmates probably continue to work dead-end jobs at best, and at worst they have succumbed to the allure of drugs, crime, and social welfare. There are exceptions—the know-nothing guy with rich parents, or the genius with no ambition—but the exceptions prove the rule.

Lynn and Vanhanen found that this anecdotal observation is supported by the data. Numerous studies and meta-analyses found that individual earnings and IQ are strongly correlated, and that this correlation increases with the degree of job difficulty. This is because more intelligent people can perform more complicated tasks, and because fewer people can perform these tasks, they command higher wages. For example, the U.S. Air Force found that 95% of candidates with IQs in the top decile completed their training, compared with only 20% of candidates with IQs in the bottom decile.

More importantly, Lynn and Vanhanen found an even stronger correlation between national average IQ and average GDP per person. They note "all the correlations between national IQs and the five measures of per capita income are positive over a 180-year period and are moderate or strong". Further, the correlations have increased since 1920. Between 1976 and 1998, after accounting for outliers, the "correlation coefficients vary from 0.725 and 0.859 and the explained part of the variation ranges from 53 to 74 percent". Therefore, the authors conclude that differences in national IQs explain over half of the variances in national wealth.[110] The authors suspect the remainder is explained by way of cultural, environmental, and institutional factors.

Lynn and Vanhanen are not the only thinkers to surmise that intelligence plays a role in economic growth. In *The Genius Famine*, Edward Dutton and Bruce Charlton note that geniuses, people of exceptional intelligence, often drive the march of history. This is because they able to shift the otherwise stagnant intellectual paradigm. For example, art history can be characterized as something of a stylistic equilibrium which is occasionally disrupted by geniuses like Michelangelo, Bernini, or Picasso.

The same is likewise true of science, industry, and economics: geniuses like Isaac Newton, Henry Ford, and Andrew Carnegie were more consequential in their respective spheres than 99.99% of humanity combined. Dutton and Charlton note that while there are many factors which allow geniuses to flourish, the most basic level society must have sufficient raw materials—a population with a sufficiently high average IQ—to generate geniuses, who are statistical outliers.

There is no question that this biological explanation of economic growth is relevant. It is an objective fact that more intelligent people usually earn higher incomes. Likewise, nations with higher average IQs tend to be richer.

However, this argument is subject to similar critiques as is the cultural explanation of economic growth. First and foremost, IQ simultaneously matters a great deal, and yet does *not* matter whatsoever. This is because Lynn and Vanhanen have made two statistical errors.

First, the data used by the authors is weighted inappropriately. On the below graph the first thing you will notice is that many European nations have been plotted. The reason for this is that Europe is divided into many different nations, each of which have a relatively high average IQ and GDP.

Unsurprisingly, IQ and wealth are found to be strongly correlated based on this data. However, Russia and China also have relatively high IQs, but have low GDPs. Nevertheless, the correlation remains because these are just two countries—one could consider them statistical outliers.

The problem with this approach is that Russia and China are orders of magnitude larger than most countries in Europe. Consider that Europe's population is just 605 million people. Meanwhile, 146 million live in Russia, and 1.4 *billion* live in China.

If Russia and China were weighted according to their population, we would find that IQ is actually *negatively* correlated with national wealth. Western Europe is the outlier—not Russia and China.

Figure 7.3

The Results of the Regression Analysis of Real GDP Per Capita 1998 on National IQ for 81 Countries in the Group of 81 Countries

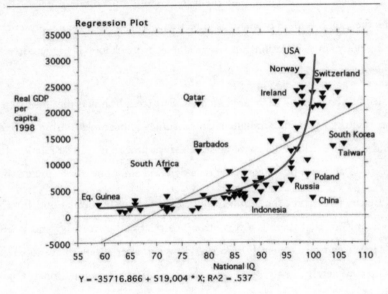

$Y = -35716.866 + 519,004 * X; R^2 = .537$

Second, Lynn and Vanhanen incorrectly assumed that there is a linear relationship between IQ and national wealth. Instead, there is clearly a *nonlinear* relationship between the two variables. A linear relationship between two variables occurs when there is a direct correlation between the two variables, and therefore a change in one variable will affect the other in a one-to-one way.

This sort of relationship generates a straight line when plotted on a graph, hence its name. Linear relationships are often found in simple systems. For example, the relationship between the number of hours worked and income earned is typically a linear relationship—work more hours, make more money.

Conversely, a nonlinear relationship between two variables occurs when there is not a direct proportional relationship between the two variables. Therefore, a change in one variable will affect the other in different ways, depending upon where we are in the graph. This sort of relationship generates a curve when plotted on a graph. Nonlinear relationships are typically found in complex systems. Further, they typically contain a parabolic shift—a point where the graph suddenly changes direction. This shift often represents a "tipping point" in the relationship, where a new feedback loop is triggered, or an emergent property changes the rules.

In the above graph there are two lines. The straight line is the "line of best fit" provided by Lynn and Vanhanen. This assumes a linear relationship between IQ and wealth. I added the curved line, which assumes a nonlinear relationship between IQ and wealth. Clearly, the data demand a nonlinear interpretation.

Let us reinterpret the graph in light of a nonlinear correlation. First, it appears obvious that there is a very strong correlation between IQ and wealth at the lower end of national IQ scores. However, after about 93 IQ this relationship completely dissolves—there is no correlation between national IQ and wealth. In this way, IQ both matters and does not matter whatsoever.

THE WISDOM OF SCROOGE MCDUCK

Thinkers throughout the ages have attempted to answer the core question of economics: "how do countries get rich". There have been many approaches to this question.

Adam Smith argues the division of labor increases productivity, and therefore specialization and capital accumulation drives economic growth. Jared Diamond focuses his explanation on environmental factors, and how they shaped historical societies. Others, like Thucydides and Max Weber surmised that cultural differences account for the wealth or poverty of different nations. Finally, Richard Lynn contends that biology—in particular IQ intelligence—drives economic growth.

While all of these explanations have something to offer, they are incomplete. In all models, long run economic growth is an exogenous condition which just magically happens in the right conditions. Yes, conditions matter. But what does economic growth actually mean? What causes it on a mechanistic level?

Economic growth is not a black box. How economic growth works, and what causes economic growth, is deceptively simple and can be summarized in one word: technology. Economic growth is simply a function of technological improvement, and the only way to grow the economy in the long run is to continuously deploy better technology. Let us work through the logic.

The economy grows when it produces more value in the same amount of time. Value can only be created in two ways: first, by making *more* output; second, by making *better* output. For example, pretend that Robinson Crusoe is shipwrecked on yet another deserted island. Having been in this predicament before, Crusoe wastes no time. During the first year of his extended "vacation" he grows 1,000 lbs of tomatoes and makes a raft out of driftwood.

In the second year, Crusoe grows 1,500 lbs of tomatoes and makes a dugout canoe. Crusoe may be unlucky, but he is certainly not lazy! Not only did Crusoe grow 50% more tomatoes, but his dugout canoe is also 50% more seaworthy. As a result, Crusoe grew the economy of his tropical paradise by 50%.

This was done by making more output, the tomatoes, and better output, the canoe. The real economy works the same way. America's GDP only increases if we make more output, like building more cars, or better output, like building better cars—they could be faster, more luxurious, or more fuel-efficient.

There are only two ways to make more output: first, we could work *harder*; second, we could work *smarter*.

Working harder simply means increasing the number of hours spend making more output. This is typically the way output was increased historically. For example, if Caesar needs more wheat, then his slaves sow more fields. If he wants more swords, then he builds another forage. If he wants to expand the forum, then his architects work through the night. In all cases, the common ingredient is to add human labor, either by hiring more workers or laboring for longer hours.

Working harder will cause economic growth, but it has three obvious drawbacks. First, no one wants to work longer hours. Second, economic growth is linear because there is a one-to-one relationship between the additional input, hours worked, and output, stuff made. That is, if one worker builds one sword per hour, then working one extra hour will create one extra sword; five extra hours will create five extra swords. Unfortunately, there are only so many hours in a day.

Third, the labor pool is only so big—eventually you will run out of collective hours in the day, and workers in the country. At this point, the only way to grow the economy further is to enslave your countrymen, or demand tribute from foreign nations. In addition to the obvious moral problems, this method cannot sustain long run economic growth. Again, there are only so many places and peoples that can be conquered in an economic way.

The second option is to work *smarter*, that is, doing more work in the same amount of time. In other words: increasing productivity. Adam Smith correctly noted that increasing productivity is the key to unlocking lasting economic growth. There are two reasons for this. First, productivity gains are often nonlinear, or exponential.

Just consider how the invention of the forklift made stevedores—the guys who load and unload cargo from ships—over 200 times as efficient as when they had to unload a ship's cargo by hand. Likewise, during the Industrial Revolution, British weavers were able to weave 40 times as much cloth after the factories deployed the power loom. [111]

These inventions alone created more economic growth than adding labor ever could. Second, there is no limit on a worker's productivity—other than our own ability to invent new technologies. Real long run economic growth depends on improving productivity. Therefore, the relevant question is this: *how do we increase productivity?*

There are a few ways to increase worker productivity. For example, workers could get more education and experience. After all, a Michelin Star chef can produce more—and more valuable (tastier)—food than a home cook. Likewise, workers could improve their productivity by taking stimulants, like drinking coffee or smoking tobacco—I could have written this book much faster if I were in a caffeine-induced fervor the whole time. At this point I greatly regret not drinking more tea.

Classical economists, like Adam Smith, argue that long run productivity gains are explained by increased division of labor, and the accumulation of more productivity-boosting capital. David Ricardo argued that these gains could be increased by trading with foreign nations with productivity asymmetries.

While there is no question that the division of labor does increase productivity—remember that Henry Ford's assembly line allowed him to make more Model T's while dropping their price—these gains are limited. This is because labor can only be divided so much before there are "too many cooks in the kitchen" and productivity or quality drops. In the end, the *only* way to increase productivity, and make more stuff, in the long run is to deploy *new productivity-boosting technology*, like forklifts or robots.

Technology is also the key to making better, more valuable, output. For example, in the 1960s computers were so large that they took up entire rooms. Today, your iPhone is more powerful than yesterday's largest supercomputers, and it fits in the palm of your hand. This is possible because of radical improvements in technology. Perhaps unsurprisingly, the highest profit margins are to be found in businesses that invent or adopt new technologies, relative to their competitors. Profits flow to the first mover, and follow and S-shaped curve.[112]

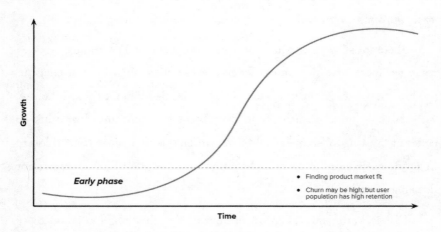

Perhaps equally unsurprisingly, this logic holds true at the national level. According to Lynn and Vanhanen, economic data shows that people living in the Netherlands, USA, and UK benefited from incomes much higher than their respective national IQ scores would predict. The reason for this is that these nations were early leaders in the Industrial Revolution. Based on standard economic models, one would have assumed that these large residuals would have declined over time due to the principle of convergence. However, this positive residual persists to this day. They found similar residuals respecting other Western European nations like France, Austria, and Sweden.

This residual is simply explained by the technological virtuous cycle: the people most likely to invent or adopt new technology are those with access to the previous generation of technology. [113] Further, the persistence of these positive residuals over centuries just go to show that this cycle is a powerful organic system that cannot be easily duplicated or moved—the virtuous cycle itself is an emergent property that generates wealth beyond what would be predicted from a nation's resources.

Technology grows the economy by allowing us to make more output, and better output, in the same amount of time. At its heart, economic growth is little more than the story of man's insatiable pursuit of knowledge from Eden to the universe's edge. It is the record of our inventions and innovations—the choicest fruit of our spirit's infinite creativity—the physical manifestation of humanity's greatest minds.

HUNTING THE BLACK SWAN

Long run economic growth is the result of technological growth. No more. No less. Therefore, if we want to grow the economy, we need to answer a new question: "how do we improve technology?"

Unfortunately, there is no *necessary* answer to this question. That is, no one factor determines when and where someone will invent something, nor can it guarantee that said invention will increase productivity. Instead, consequential inventions are *black swans* which we can forecast, but not predict.

In *The Black Swan*, Nassim Taleb argues that complex systems—and much of the natural world—are typically governed by black swan events. That is, highly improbable yet highly consequential events. This is not an intuitive concept, so we will run through two examples to make it clear.

First, we will consider an example from the natural world. Hundreds of earthquakes occur under our feet daily. Most of these earthquakes cannot be detected without special equipment, and therefore are of no consequence. Even those earthquakes that are perceptible usually do little more than shake the chandeliers.

However, roughly once a century the "big one" hits, causing massive destruction and chaos in its wake. In this way, 0.1% of earthquakes cause almost all the damage caused by earthquakes. Importantly, it is *impossible* to predict earthquakes. At best, seismologists can forecast when and where big earthquakes are most likely to occur.

For our second example of a black swan event, consider the printing press. In approximately 1440 Johannes Gutenberg, a German goldsmith, built a printing press which had moveable type. That is, the printing press could be "reprogrammed" with different text at will. This invention allowed Gutenberg to print some 3,600 pages of text per day. This was an enormous improvement over scribes, who could manually copy just 40 pages per day.

Gutenberg's printing press made the printing industry 90 times as efficient—virtually overnight. Not only did this create wealth by increasing productivity, but the widespread availability of books changed transformed society itself. It is not an understatement to say that the modern world owes its existence to the humble Johannes Gutenberg.

The example of Gutenberg's printing press tells us three important things about black swan events. First, they are rare. Gutenberg's printing press was invented around 1440—over 2,000 years after the West developed a literate society which demanded books. Likewise, true moveable type presses were invented only twice in human history, once in Europe and once in China.

Second, black swan events are consequential. The Gutenberg press made bookmakers 90 more efficient. The printing press changed how we process and store information more than any previous or subsequent inventions, with the exception of the alphabet itself.

Third, we cannot predict when a black swan event will occur. Why did Gutenberg invent the printing press in 1440? Why not in 1460? Why was this not invented in Ancient Rome or Medieval Constantinople? Why was it invented to begin with? After all, Europeans had faired perfectly well without the printing press for thousands of years. There really is no answer to this question, other than to recognize the role that the chance and individual people play in human history.

At this point, I will forgive you if you have thrown your hands up in exasperation—what good is it to know that black swan events drive long run economic growth if they are simply the product of dumb luck? While we may be at the mercy of chance, there are steps we can take to maximize the economy's exposure to positive black swan events. We can tip the odds in our favor.

ON THE NECESSITY OF THIRST

One of Aesop's most famous fables is the 'The Crow and the Pitcher'. In this fable, a thirsty crow sees a pitcher of water. The crow tries to drink, but her beak is not long enough to reach the water. The clever crow then drops a pebble in the pitcher. The water level rises. The crow drops pebbles into the pitcher again and again, until she can drink freely. The moral of this story?

Necessity is the mother of invention.

Aesop was right. Just as the crow's desire to drink motivated her to invent a way to reach the water, so too does man's desire to fulfill his needs and wants fuels his creative spirit. As such, *necessity* is the first factor which increases the likelihood of breeding black swans. Economic necessity is primarily created by competition between different economic entities.

This competition is fractal, and occurs between different individuals, business, and states simultaneously. At the individual level people compete for money, power, fame—status. While most people compete by working harder, some work smarter by finding ways to increase their productivity, and therefore their incomes.

Consider the example of Titian (d. 1576). Titian was a Venetian painter who is considered by most art historians to be one of the "Great Masters". This accolade is warranted not only because the quality of Titian's portraiture, but because of his sheer volume. To this day, Titian remains one of the West's most prolific—and richest—artists. Was this because Titian worked harder than his contemporaries? No. Titian found a way to work smarter.

Titian devised a system that was somewhat akin to an assembly line for portraits, wherein different artists at his workshop were responsible for different aspects of the art. For example, one artist may specialize in painting eyes while another specialized in painting hair. Titian oversaw the process, and would typically prepare the rough sketches and final touch-ups himself. In this way, Titian was able to outcompete his rivals, surpassing them in both fame and fortune.

Competition is fractal and occurs simultaneously at multiple levels of organization. Businesses compete ruthlessly for market share. This competition drives invention and innovation. For example, during the Industrial Revolution in Great Britain, businesses were engaged in ruthless competition with one another. In 1786 Edmund Cartwright invented the *power loom*, a mechanical weaving machine which allowed British textile workers to produce 40 times as much cloth as workers using hand looms. As a result, factories which adopted the power loom could not only produce significantly more cloth, but they could do so for a fraction of the price.

Competition between British textile companies made it not just profitable, but *necessary*, for their competitors to upgrade their factories. In 1803 there were 2,400 power looms in Great Britain. This number increased exponentially: in 1820 there were 14,650 power looms, and by 1829 there were 55,500. The number of power looms in Great Britain peaked in 1857 at 250,000. Competition drove Britain's textile industry to boost productivity by increasing technology and accumulating capital. As a result, Great Britain became the world's richest nation and the first to industrialize.

Finally, competition at the state level can create economic necessity. Further, the sheer scale of state competition often increases competition on all other levels. The greatest example of this is World War II, which pitted the Axis and Allied powers in existential competition.

The result was the widespread adoption of underutilized technologies, and the invention of entirely new products. Consider that the British scientist Alexander Fleming discovered penicillin in 1928, however, it was not until the war that penicillin was mass-produced. After the war, the drug was made available for civilians, and changed the healthcare industry forever.

Other key technologies which were developed include jet engines, radar, computers, rockets, and nuclear fission. These technologies went on to revolutionize the modern world, and there is no guarantee that they would have been developed were it not for the necessities created by the war.

Consider that the gas turbine was first patented in England by John Barber in 1791. Nothing came of this discovery until Frank Whittle, a Royal Air Force engineer, invented the modern jet engine in the lead-up to the war. The first allied jet plane took flight in on May 15, 1941. Likewise, rockets had been used in European warfare since at least the Fourteenth Century. However, it was the existential necessities created by the Second World War, and the ensuing Cold War, which escalated rocket development, giving us intercontinental ballistic missiles and rocket ships. State competition—not competition between individuals or corporations—fueled the space race.

IN PRAISE OF CROWS

Necessity is the mother of invention, but man remains the father. Accordingly, competition will not increase the likelihood of black swans without the proper raw materials—without the right kind of men.

The type of men who drive economic growth, and who make countries rich, have three things in common: first, they are *intelligent* enough to solve problems; second, they have a creative and independent *personality* which allows them to question the norm; and third, they are *knowledgeable* enough to identify problems and invent practical solutions.

Human intelligence is required to generate long run economic growth. Let us return to Aesop's fable 'The Crow and the Pitcher'. Water is a *necessity* for the thirsty crow. This necessity drives the crow to think of a creative solution to quench her thirst. However, we cannot forget that this fable only makes sense because the crow herself is smart enough to solve the problem.

Imagine if instead of a crow, the fable featured an earthworm. Would the earthworm be smart enough to solve this problem? No. An earthworm is stupid. It would die of thirst. Aesop shows us the importance of both *necessity* and *intelligence.*

Lynn and Vanhannen's data demonstrates that that nations with average IQs below 93 are almost uniformly poor. Conversely, nations with IQs above 93 are both rich and poor in roughly equal measure. The reason for this is that the modern economy is not just a complex system, it is also a system filled with complexity.

Only people with sufficient intelligence can organize complex supply chains or operate complex technologies. Countries with insufficient IQs simply do not have enough people with the requisite intelligence to maintain a modern economy—never mind invent or deploy the technologies which drive long-run economic growth. The following thought experiment makes this abundantly clear.

There are two towns. Sunnyvale and Cambridge. The average inhabitant of Sunnyvale has an IQ of 75, and looks suspiciously like Ricky from *Trailer Park Boys*. If you have not seen this series, Ricky is like Kramer from *Seinfeld*— if Kramer was a violent alcoholic, pothead, and jailbird. Meanwhile, the average inhabitant of Cambridge has an IQ of 125, and carries himself with the dour resolution of Isaac Newton. Which town is likely to be richer?

Will it be Sunnyvale, where the average inhabitant thinks the phrase "kill two birds with one stone" is actually "get two birds stoned at once"? Or Cambridge, where the average inhabitant *enjoys* calculus? Which town is more likely to repair engines with duct tape? Which town is more likely to invent a new kind of duct tape?

Intelligence matters. Everyone knows this, even if they do not have the courage to admit it. A nation with more intelligent people simply has more people who are able to deploy complex solutions, and solve complex problems. This enriches the entire nation, and everyone in the nation—from Ricky to Isaac—benefits.

THE KOBAYASHI MARU PRINCIPLE

In *The Wrath of Khan*, every cadet enrolled in the Starfleet Academy must confront the Kobayashi Maru scenario—a no-win situation. Starfleet Academy cadets were directed to rescue the Kobayashi Maru, a civilian fuel ship, which was stranded in neutral territory between the Federation and the Klingons. When they tried to do so, they would be attacked by an insurmountable force and destroyed. The best and brightest cadets all failed. However, James T. Kirk found a creative way to cheat the system and win. Although Kirk was less academic than some of his competitors, his independent *personality* allowed him to invent a creative solution to the problem—a problem for which no solution was possible.

This brings us to my second point: economic growth also requires enough people with the right personality traits.

Dutton and Charlton note that *intelligence* boils down to brain efficiency—how fast the brain processes information. Meanwhile, *personality* describes what the brain is designed to do. If we compare the brain to a computer, intelligence is the hardware and personality is the software. With the exception of *openness*, personality traits are not consistently correlated with IQ. Intelligence and personality are categorically different metrics.

Psychologists often describe personality using the "Big 5" personality traits, which are summarized below:

(1) *Conscientiousness* refers to a person's ability to adhere to social norms, by regulating impulses and persevering in goal-oriented behaviors. Highly conscientious people like to be prepared, stick to schedules, and follow the rules. They are engaged with the social system, and help to maintain it. Often these sorts of people gravitate to careers that prize organization and attention to detail, like physicians, politicians, or bookkeepers.

Some good examples of conscientious characters from pop culture include Monica Geller from *Friends*, Hermione Granger from *Harry Potter*, or Cogsworth from Disney's *Beauty and the Beast*. Unsurprisingly, conscientiousness is correlated with economic success at the individual level—consistency is king in the nine-to-five grind.

On the other hand, people who are not conscientious tend to be more impulsive. Often, they will obsess over something that personally interests them, at the expense of their other social obligations. Doc Brown from *Back to the Future* is a good example of someone who is both smart, but not very conscientious.

(2) *Extroversion* refers to a person's need for external—usually social—stimulation. Highly extroverted people gravitate towards social activities, enjoy meeting new people, and maintaining social networks. These types of people often excel as criminal defense lawyers, teachers, and salesmen. Princess Leia from *Star Wars* or Boromir from the *Lord of the Rings* are classic examples of extroverts.

Extroversion is also highly correlated with economic success at the individual level. In fact, in their book *Connected*, James H. Fowler and Nicholas Christakis showed that the size and diversity of an individual's social network was actually the most important predictor of said individual's economic success—it was even more important than their IQ.

On the other hand, an introvert does not seek social gratification and praise. Instead, they are internally-motivated to pursue their own interests. Pop culture examples include Walter White from *Breaking Bad* or Bilbo Baggins from *The Hobbit*.

(3) *Openness* refers to a person's willingness to try new things, and to engage in imaginative or creative activities. People who are highly open are curious, interested in novelty, and often enjoy creative pastimes. Good examples of this trait include Alice from *Alice in Wonderland* and Luke Skywalker from *Star Wars*.

Interestingly, openness is the only personality trait which is consistently correlated with IQ—both at the individual and national level. There is a weak relationship between openness and economic success at the individual level, although it is difficult to isolate this variable.

(4) *Neuroticism* describes a person's emotional stability, and how they perceive the world. People with high neuroticism often have a "negative" view of the world, and this may manifest with depression, anxiety, and mood swings in response to changing stimuli. This is, in part, because they tend to feel negative emotions very strongly.

A classic example of a highly neurotic character is C-3PO from *Star Wars*. Meanwhile, Han Solo would be on the opposite side of this spectrum. Although this trait is not directly linked to personal economic success, the way in which it interplays with other personality traits is important.

(5) *Agreeableness* describes an individual's empathetic interest in other people. While the extrovert seeks social stimulation—sometimes in a solipsistic or narcissistic way—a genuinely agreeable person displays empathy, altruism, and reciprocal trust. On the other hand, a "disagreeable" person is more likely to focus on objective ideas, systems, or facts, rather than concentrate on people's subjective feelings.

Examples of agreeable characters include many Disney princesses like Belle from *Beauty and the Beast* or Snow White from, well, *Snow White*. Meanwhile, disagreeable characters include blockbuster icons like Anakin Skywalker, Indiana Jones, and James Bond.

Although these personality traits are not strongly correlated with IQ, they are correlated with each other. J. Philippe Rushton showed that they can be reasonably approximated by a single variable, *general factor personality*. Essentially, this measures the degree to which an individual is pro-social, whether they have an *exogenous* personality.[114]

Given that personality traits like conscientiousness, extroversion, and openness are all strongly correlated with individual income and personal success, it seems logical to assume that they are also correlated with national wealth. It also seems reasonable to infer that societies with pro-social populations are richer than those with more asocial or anti-social personalities. However, this is not the case.

The *only* personality trait which is consistently correlated with national wealth is extroversion. This is likely because extraversion is the social lubrication that allows groups of people to organize their labor, and exchange goods and knowledge. Interestingly, the other personality traits are not correlated with national wealth. In fact, some researchers have even found *negative* correlations between "helpful" traits, like conscientious, and national wealth.[115]

Perhaps more puzzling is the fact that there are no negative correlations between asocial personality traits, like high degrees of neuroticism or introversion, and national wealth. How can it be that personality traits which make individuals richer, do not also make countries richer? This is a paradox.

Dutton and Charlton have proposed that historical progress—political, artistic, and technological—is driven primarily by *geniuses*—human black swans. Geniuses are people who are both extraordinarily intelligent, and have an *endogenous* personality. That is, they have the mental hardware to solve complex problems, and their mental software predisposes them to enjoy solving hard problems—even at the expense of their social reputation or personal success.

An exogenous personality is pro-social. An endogenous personality, on the other hand, is asocial or anti-social. That is, they are either not particularly interested in fitting-in with the rest of society, or they actively reject social norms. Someone with an endogenous personality typically scores low on conscientiousness, extraversion, and agreeableness, and high on openness and neuroticism. Let us put aside the scientific jargon for a second, and instead describe the genius personality in more practical ways.

To begin with, geniuses score relatively low on conscientiousness. Essentially, they have trouble regulating their impulses. This results in geniuses foregoing daily routines and social activities to pursue their obsessions—obsessions which may not have any immediate value to the genius, or even to society at large.

For example, Isaac Newton—who invented physics and calculus—lived a life of complete disarray. His offices at Cambridge were chronically messy. Often, he would go abnormally long periods without so much as eating or bathing. Instead, he was entirely fixated on whatever problem he was trying to solve at the time.

Geniuses also score relatively high on openness. This means the genius is interested in the world around him. He is curious, and eager to absorb new information. A high score on this trait is unsurprising. What may be more surprising is the high score on neuroticism. In the case of geniuses, this trait typically manifests as a tendency to dwell and obsess on a problem until they can figure out a solution. For example, Leonardo Da Vinci famously worked on painting the Mona Lisa's lips for twelve years until he was satisfied.

Geniuses score relatively low on extraversion. As we have seen, extraverted people are energized by external stimulation. On the other side of the spectrum, introverted people are energized to pursue their own personal interests. They are internally motivated. What this means in practice is that introverts are much more likely to spend their time solving "boring" problems, than they are to compete for social prestige.

Finally—and perhaps most importantly—geniuses tend to score low on agreeableness. That is, they are more interested in understanding facts than they are about hurting people's feelings. This allows geniuses to think taboo thoughts, and to consider ideas that are outside of the box.

A good example of a disagreeable genius is Galileo Galilei. Galileo believed that the earth revolved around the sun, and spent his life proving this point. Although he was arrested multiple times, and excommunicated from the Catholic Church (not necessarily for his beliefs, but primarily for being disagreeable), Galileo persisted. No amount of social pressure was strong enough to overcome Galileo's stubbornness.

To summarize: geniuses are highly intelligent and typically have endogenous personalities. Rather than seeking social validation, geniuses are internally-motivated—often to an obsessive degree—to solve problems that they find interesting. Moreover, they are open to thinking outside the box, and are willing to stand by their ideas in the face of staunch social pressures.[viii]

It is self-evident that geniuses are responsible for mankind's greatest technological breakthroughs, and therefore economic growth. Remember, almost all game-changing technologies were invented by individual people—they were by no means inevitable, nor did they seem obvious until *after* they were invented.

The process of technological "evolution" is only obvious to us in hindsight. This is why our predictions of what the future will look like are *always* spectacularly *wrong*. We simply cannot envision "obvious" technologies before they are actually invented. Need proof? Read Jules Verne or H.G. Wells.

---

viii Interestingly, the endogenous personality type is tied to testosterone levels—the higher the testosterone levels in a society, the more people (usually men) will have endogenous personality types. In particular, high levels of testosterone are linked to decreased agreeableness and conscientiousness, and to neurodivergences like psychopathy and autism, which generally conform within the endogenous personality parameters.

In a recent study, Edward Dutton et al. examined the rates of Nobel Prizes and scientific publications per capita by country. After accounting for differences in intelligence, the researchers found that differences in national testosterone levels (as estimated based on a host of proxy markers), explained 67% of differences in the above scientific achievements between countries. All of this is to say that that national testosterone levels may be a useful took for discovering where endogenous personalities can be found.

https://onlinelibrary.wiley.com/doi/abs/10.1002/jocb.351

The reason for this is that most people lack the enormous intelligence needed to solve the big problems faced by geniuses. Further, most people who are sufficiently intelligent have exogenous personalities, and as such use their intellects to obtain status—fame, wealth, and power—rather than solving intellectual problems in anonymity.

This may explain why nations with highly exogenous aggregate personalities—pro-social nations like China or Japan—are not as wealthy or inventive as European nations, whose populations have more people with endogenous personalities—despite their similar national IQs.[ix] It is not enough to be smart; you must also have an independent mind.

A comparison of Julius Caesar and Isaac Newton shows the differences that personalities make. To begin with, Julius Caesar and Isaac Newton were among the most intelligent men of their respective eras.

Caesar was a brilliant military strategist and statesman, who used his towering intellect to conquer Gaul, Egypt, and win the Roman Civil War against Pompey the Great—who had himself subdued most of the Greek speaking world. Caesar's name became synonymous with emperor, living on as the Roman Caesar, German Kaiser, and Russian Czar. Although Caesar was certainly intelligent enough to invent technologies, his personality drove

---

ix Like intelligence, personality traits are largely hereditable. In fact, Dutton and Charlton show that approximately 50 - 70% of a person's personality is determined by their genes. Personality is relevant on both the individual and national level.

Although not referenced in their work, a good example of genes driving personality traits and behavior is a gene allele called DRD4. This gene is involved with dopamine receptors and makes them fire more in response to novel stimuli and reports. This allele results in "hyperexcitability, strong novelty and reward seeking, and a tendency to adapt to arousing experiences fast and thus be ready for more". People with this gene are more likely to have ADHD, do recreational drugs, and engage in other novelty and risk-seeking behavior.

Interestingly, research from Robert Moyzis of the University of California found that the prevalence of this gene varies across human populations, and it has since been dubbed the "migration gene". This gene is almost extinct in Africa and China, but is carried by approximately 25% of Western Europeans. The prevalence of this gene may help to explain why Europe—and not China—was responsible for creating the vast majority of humanity's art and science, despite China's similar national average IQ and much larger population. For further reading on this topic, see *New* by Winifred Gallagher (pp. 53 – 66).

him into the social arena. He was highly extroverted and conscientious, and dedicated his life to engaging with society.

Conversely, Isaac Newton was notoriously asocial—or perhaps more appropriately, anti-social. Newton was internally motivated to pursue his own esoteric interests, like physics, mathematics, and theology. His relentless pursuit of his own introverted goals made him a social pariah, although this did not seem to bother Newton. In the end, Newton was able to elucidate the laws of physics, he discovered the properties of light, and he invented calculus. While both Caesar and Newton were enormously intelligent, their different personalities directed their intelligence in the pursuit of very different goals.

Perhaps the most important lesson that we can learn from a comparison of Caesar and Newton is that black swan events are by no means inevitable, but are the products of individual genius. Although Caesar conquered Gaul, this event was not inevitable. The Romans had failed to conquer Gaul for centuries—in fact, Gallic tribes had themselves sacked Rome in the past. The fact that Rome conquered Gaul is a historical black swan event caused by Julius Caesar.

Likewise, the creation of calculus was by no means inevitable. Remember, the theoretical problem solved by calculus had been known by western mathematicians since at least the days of Zeno of Elea (d. 430 B.C.). It took humanity 2,000 years to solve this problem. It took Newton a matter of months. Geniuses matter.

NO ZODIAC, NO CALCULUS

I find the idea of Zodiac signs predicting our personalities to be foolish—but as a Scorpio I would say that.

To me, the constellations are interesting for a different reason. Namely, they prove that knowledge precedes creativity. Imagine you are nearsighted. You look up at the night sky and you can only see the twinkling of the brightest half of the stars. Although the sky is beautiful, all you see are individual stars glimmering through the blackness—you cannot see any connections between them because you cannot see enough stars.

A week later you buy a pair of glasses and can see all the starts. You look up at the sky again, and this time notice that some stars appear to form patterns in the sky. You see one that looks like a man with a bow, Orion, and another that looks like a ladle, the Big Dipper. Only after you could see the stars were you able to connect the dots, and "create" a constellation.

The sort of human creativity that leads to technological invention, and thereby long run economic growth, requires not only sufficient intelligence and the right kind of personality, but it also requires *knowledge*. Knowledge refers to the level of information, usually gained through education or experience, remembered by an individual. Importantly, knowledge is sequentially path-dependent—it builds on what came before.

This is why we do not even attempt to teach children calculus in elementary school: a student *cannot* learn calculus until they have learned algebra, which itself would make no sense to a student who did not know how to add or multiply numbers. Likewise, a student who *only* just learned how to add and multiply numbers could not then invent calculus, because they would simply not have enough knowledge to even recognize the problem. Simply put, they do not understand enough mathematical concepts—they do not see enough stars—to discover calculus—to see a constellation.

Lynn and Vanhannen noted that between 1820 and 1992 certain nations, like the Netherlands, France, the UK, and USA, were consistently richer than their IQ scores would predict. They hypothesize that this was because these nations were early "leaders in industrialization and technological development", and these early advantages continued to benefit these economies in subsequent centuries. Lynn and Vanhannen are basically correct: these nations remained technologically advanced and rich because they were already technologically advanced and rich.

This makes intuitive sense. For example, pretend there are ten people in a room. Nine of them are in grade school. One is Isaac Newton. Which person is most likely to make a mathematical discovery? Obviously, Isaac Newton.

The children will not be able to discover anything that Newton does not already know, or could not himself discover, until they at least know as much as him. And unfortunately for the students, if Newton continues to learn at the same rate as them, they will *never* catch up with Newton and *never* discover anything new. Newton's early advantage in knowledge virtually guarantees that he will make every new discovery—and reap the according economic benefits.

This is exactly what has occurred at the national level. The most technologically advanced nations in 1820 remain among the most technologically advanced nations today, and are responsible for inventing most new technologies over the same period. For example, the steam engine, internal combustion engine, trains, planes, automobiles, electricity, the light bulb, the telephone, satellites and interplanetary rockets, nuclear fission, penicillin, televisions, computers, and the internet were all invented in Europe or her colonies—mostly in the UK and USA.

Conversely, nations which have relatively lower levels of technology like China, Ireland, and Poland, invented relatively little in terms of paradigm-shifting technology, and remained relatively poor until recently—despite their similar national IQ scores.

Knowledge builds on knowledge, and technology builds on technology. Therefore, nations which deploy relatively high levels of technology not only maximize their economic productivity in the present, but they also increase the likelihood that new technologies will be discovered, which leads to productivity gains tomorrow.

We talked about how offshoring is a vicious cycle which undermines economic growth. Technological growth is the opposite: it is a *virtuous cycle* wherein every discovery makes the next discovery more likely. This not only helps explain why some countries are rich and others poor, but why rich countries usually stay rich and poor countries usually stay poor.

OF WATSON AND KOROLEV

In addition to the "raw materials" of intelligence, personality, and knowledge, there are three other factors worth mentioning which increase the likelihood of the sort of black swan events which cause technological, and therefore economic, growth. This list is not exhaustive.

The psychological roots of human creativity are not well understood, and new ways to increase human creativity may be discovered. For example, research into nootropics is a burgeoning industry which may yield pharmaceuticals which help boost creativity. That said, these are the most important "big picture" historical factors.

The first factor is *freedom*. Freedom means that individuals have the latitude to identify problems, think of solutions to those problems, and to manufacture or implement those solutions. To be clear, I am *not* talking about political freedom. Although there is often significant overlap between political freedom and the sort of freedom required to facilitate genius, history shows us that genius can flourish in authoritarian states and be smothered in "free" societies. As usual, an example will help clarify this point.

James Watson was awarded the 1962 Nobel Prize in Physiology or Medicine for co-discovering the DNA double helix. This research allowed humanity to decipher the "language" of life, which has significant practical applications in the scientific fields ranging from medicine to anthropology. Until recently, Watson was a towering intellectual figure with a flourishing career: he helped found the Human Genome Project and was actively involved in a number of other more recent projects.

In 2007, Watson stated in an interview that differences in average behavior and intelligence between ethnic groups was caused by differences in their DNA. Watson was accused of racism. His comments ultimately led to his "retirement" from his own lab, which cut all ties with him and revoked his honorary titles. Watson was essentially unable to conduct further research or participate in the scientific discourse. Watson was "cancelled", and America rejected one of her most acclaimed scientists.

Watson is far from the only scientist who has been lynched by the media in recent years. Consider that Charles Murray, whose 1994 book *The Bell Curve: Intelligence and Class Structure in American Life* has shaped two generations of subsequent sociological scholarship, has been viciously targeted by both the media and political "activists" who have threatened his personal safety. Even Richard Lynn, whose work has been referenced at length in this book, has been the victim of the "Cancel Culture" movement. Disturbingly, this process is not new.

Since the 1970s America's university campuses have been purged of conservative professors. In 1999 the Carnegie Foundation found that just 12% of professors were conservatives, down from 27% in 1969. This number has continued to decline—especially in the humanities. For example, as of 2014 conservatives make up just 4% of historians, 3% of sociologists, and 2% of literature professors.

Overall, 11.7% of professors teaching at private universities are conservative, and just 7.7% of professors at public universities are conservative. Further, these conservative professors were not replaced by independents, but by increasingly dedicated leftists.[116] This is entirely at odds with the political views of the American public, which has actually grown *more* conservative over the same time period, once the views of first-generation immigrants are accounted for.

The purging of conservatives from university campuses has caused intellectual stagnation. Certain areas of research—such as the genetic basis for human intelligence and personality—are effectively banned topics. Likewise, America's universities have become echo chambers wherein dissent is not only socially discouraged, it simply does not exist.

This has a chilling effect on the ability of independently minded professors and students to identify problems and come up with creative solutions, for fear that their observations or hypotheses may result in their being cancelled. After all, if a Nobel Prize winning scientist like James Watson can be ruined, what hope is there for a lowly graduate student? Further, the lack of conservative professors has deprived universities with intellectual competition—and as we saw, competition is the driving force behind human creativity.

On paper, America is one of the world's freest societies. Americans have constitutionally protected rights to speak freely, own property, and protest their government. However, these political freedoms have little to do with the type of freedoms required to facilitate creativity. For example, the USSR led the Space Race up until 1969 when America landed on the moon. The USSR was the first nation to launch an artificial satellite into orbit, the first to launch an animal, a man, and a woman into space, and the first nation to build a space station.

These impressive scientific and industrial feats were accomplished by one of the nations with the *least* political freedom in human history. How did the USSR accomplish this? Ironically, it is because the USSR permitted its Chief Engineer, Sergei Korolev (d. 1966), the intellectual freedom to identify problems, think of solutions to the problems, and then manufacture those solutions. Essentially, the USSR recognized Korolev's genius, afforded him the right kind of freedom to indulge his creativity, and reaped the benefits.

The lessons from the above examples are that if we want to increase the likelihood of black swan events, and therefore technological and economic growth, then we must provide our people—particularly our best and brightest—with the right kind of freedom. Ironically, we do not need more political freedom. Nor do we need freedom in a hedonistic, libertarian, sense; the right to smoke marijuana and snort cocaine are not related to the production of geniuses. Instead, Americans must be free to identify problems, to come up with creative solutions from said problems, and to manufacture or implement these solutions.

The best way to allow Americans to identify problems is to embrace unrestricted free speech. A good start could be extending the "town square" principle onto social media platforms and internet service providers, and to increase protections for tenured professors. This would open the Overton Window, and allow for greater diversity of thought, which in turn would de-stigmatize dissident opinions.

Another option would be for America to break up multinational conglomerates, prohibit large mergers and acquisitions, and reorient economic policy to support local businesses. The reason for this is that smaller businesses are less likely to be subject to group think, and competition between smaller companies will inherently limit the ability of companies to police an inventive employee's thoughts—he could just jump ship and join another company, and his departure would be a proportionally bigger blow. The same logic applies at the state level: decentralizing the federal government would empower the states and people proportionately.

Although the government can do more to protect its citizen's rights to free speech, most intellectual suppression is done by private organizations like universities, the media, and multinational corporations. As such, it is much more difficult to offer concrete solutions to fix this problem.

For example, during law school I made public comments respecting the way in which western governments mishandled the flood of refugees associated with Syrian Civil War. A number of disgruntled students confronted me regarding my comments. I was kindly asked to publicly retract my statements and apologize. My understanding is that a number of these students likewise approached the Dean of the Faculty of Law in a vain attempt to pressure me into thinking the right sort of thoughts. I stood firm and nothing came of their accusations.

The media and multinational companies are also actively engaged in the suppression of conservative thought. I have likewise experienced this firsthand. For example, in 2018, my online publication, the *National Economics Editorial*, was featured on a "fact checking" website. This website noted that my publication was a trumpet for "extreme right" ideology.

For clarity, most of our articles were economic in nature, and detailed our opposition to international free trade and economic globalism. Shortly thereafter, the *Editorial* was evidently delisted from Google search—we saw a 90% reduction in organic search traffic overnight. Further, the organic reach of my Facebook page, which had 84,000 followers at the time, was limited to such an extent that the page was rendered useless. I was also shadow banned from Twitter. I give these personal examples not to appear as a martyr, but to show that this sort of social suppression occurs not just to Nobel Prize-winning scientists like James Watson, but to minor intellectual figures with small follows.

The social suppression of dissenting intellectuals and ideas—which prevents the type of creativity needed to invent new technologies and grow the economy—follows a predictable pattern. First, the individual is socially shamed until he complies. If this fails, the second step is to coerce the individual into compliance by targeting their livelihood.

Third, a truly recalcitrant individual is scrubbed from the internet, as happened to Andrew Anglin in the wake of the Charlottesville protests in 2017. There is no specific policy that can cure the sickness of social suppression; however, it is possible to make citizens more robust in its face. The easiest way to do this is to grow the economy and enrich the average American.

The reason of this is that affluent citizens, who do not *need* to work to survive, have "fuck you" money—they can speak their mind without fear of economic ruination. This is why most of history's mavericks, from Alcibiades and the Gracchi Brothers to Henry Ford and Theodore Roosevelt, have been men of affluence. Slaves, serfs, and peasants simply cannot afford to speak their mind.

The economy grows when geniuses are accorded the freedom to identify problems, dream-up solutions, and to put these solutions into practice. Free speech—which is facilitated by political and economic decentralization, and protected by widespread affluence—makes the first two elements more likely.

The third element relies on a different sort of freedom: the freedom to *do*. History shows us that the best way to facilitate this sort of freedom is to paradoxically have a government which is both small and big. The economically optimal government should be small in the sense that it governs with a light touch: there should be relatively few laws or regulations, and these laws should be simple. Taxes should be relatively low and non-intrusive.

On the other hand, the government should be big, in that it enforces its laws and regulations uniformly and without delay. This is because people are more likely to invest their time and resources into creative endeavours if they know they can protect the fruits of their labor. Historically, the governments of Great Britain and the United States of America balanced these competing objectives best in the late Eighteenth through early Twentieth Centuries. Unsurprisingly, this was these nation's period of technological blossoming.

ON DA VINCI AND BIG CHUNGUS

In addition to *freedom*, there are two other factors which increase the likelihood of technological growth: *economic diversity* and *size*. Economic diversity is important for two reasons. First, diverse economies are more likely to generate and benefit from black swan events than are highly specialized economies.

This is because of the role that chance plays in economic growth. Remember, the economy is not a giant billiard's table: we cannot *know* which industries will generate or benefit from new technologies. At best, we can forecast which industries are the most likely to do so. Therefore, the best way to maximize our exposure to black swan events is to maximize the number of different industries operating within the economy. Basically, it is better to put our eggs in many different baskets and hope at least one hen will roost, as opposed to putting them all in one basket and pray for a big payoff.

Not coincidentally, this economic strategy lines up with success in the stock market. Like the economy more generally, the stock market is subject to chance—no one *knows* which stocks will outperform the market in the long run. As such, broad-based investment strategies tend to outperform those which target particular "growth" industries, or even individual stocks.

For example, the S&P Composite 1500 Index outperformed 83.76% of all actively managed investment funds over a 15-year period. Interestingly, the Index outperformed funds which targeted smaller companies—promising companies which investment managers thought would offer explosive growth— by an even wider margin. The S&P SmallCap 600 Index outperformed 97.7% of all investment funds targeting Small-Cap stocks. [117]

The second reason that diverse economies support economic growth is that they provide greater opportunities for inventors to manufacture or implement their creative solutions. That is, economic diversity helps geniuses manifest their dreams. For example, consider the contrasting stories of Leonardo Da Vinci (d.1519) and Orville and Wilbur Wright (d. 1948 and 1912 respectively).

Da Vinci was one of history's greatest geniuses. Not only was he renowned for his artistic achievements, which include his famous paintings the

Mona Lisa and the Last Supper, but Da Vinci was a polymath who theorized a number of different flying machines, including the airplane and the "aerial screw", a primitive helicopter. Of course, nothing ever came of Da Vinci's flying machines, and it was not until the Wright Brother's inaugural airplane flight of 1903 that mankind took to the skies.

There is little doubt that Da Vinci could have invented the airplane. This begs the question: why did his designs come to nothing? There are two main reasons. First, technological growth is path dependent. Da Vinci simply could not have engineered a successful airplane because the internal combustion engine had not yet been invented, and there was no equivalent source of portable power available to Da Vinci.

Da Vinci's dreams were limited by the age in which he lived. Second, it is unlikely that Da Vinci would have been able to build a working aircraft because Fifteenth Century Italy lacked the economic diversity to manufacture the required component pieces. The manufacturing of complex technologies typically requires specialized manufacturing.

The third and final factor which is relevant to an economy's probability at producing black swans is its size. It goes without saying that bigger economies are more likely to invent new technologies than are small economies—there is a reason that the USA files many more patents than does Canada or Barbados.

That said, size is not everything. There are plenty of relatively large economies with large populations, like India or Nigeria, that do not produce many new technologies. Meanwhile, some relatively small economies, like Switzerland or Singapore, produce many new technologies. This is largely because some industries are more likely to produce economic growth than others.

What matters more than the size of the overall economy is the size of its advanced industries, which employ the types of people who are most likely to invent new technologies, and grow the economy.

MEMENTO MORI

In this chapter we learned that long run economic growth is simply the offspring of technological growth. Technological growth is motivated by *necessity*, and requires a population with sufficient *intelligence*, the right *personality*, and enough *knowledge*. The right combination of these factors produces a creative society with enough people—creative geniuses, or diligent innovators—who can recognize problems, solve them, and implement their solutions.

We cannot predict when paradigm-shifting technologies will be invented, they are *black swan events*. However, we can improve the likelihood that black swans will breed. We can do this by safeguarding *freedom* and by increasing the *diversity* and *size* of the economy.

Importantly, because technological growth is path dependent, in the sense that new technologies build on older technologies, economies with the most exposure to new technologies will be the most likely to continue inventing new technologies. This *technological virtuous cycle* is the engine of long run economic growth.

This is my answer to the ultimate question of economics.

CHAPTER 9

HOW TARIFFS FIX THE PROBLEMS

The conquests of Alexander the Great (d. 323 BC) were a brilliant flash in the bleak march of history. Within just 13 years, Alexander conquered everything between the ancient Nile and the mysterious Indus. His was the greatest empire the world had ever seen.

So eclectic was Alexander's spirit, and so impressive were his deeds, that he was hailed as a descendent of Herakles in Sparta, deified as a son of Amon Ra in Egypt, and acclaimed as the Great King in Persia. Alexander the Great was all things to all people. Why?

Alexander was *practical*: he did not allow his knowledge of how things ought to work in theory with how they actually work in practice. Given Alexander's pragmatism in governing different people with different strategies, it will come as no surprise that he was tutored by Aristotle—the father of inductive reasoning, and grandfather of the scientific method.

This is in stark contrast to how Dionysius II, who with Plato's help, ruled Syracuse. If you recall, Dionysius tried to rule as a *philosopher king*: a perfectly rational and knowledgeable monarch who governed according to ideal principles, so that his kingdom better reflected the *theoretically ideal* kingdom.

Of course, the world is not rational, and Dionysius did not know as much as he thought. This is why Dionysius, like every political ideologue after him—from Robespierre to Stalin—not only failed to turn grim reality into a gleaming utopia, but often manifested Hell on earth.

In this final chapter, we will leave theory behind and instead look at a time-tested, practical way to fix America's broken economy: *tariffs*.

To start, I will explain what tariffs are and how they work. Next, I will show you that tariffs have been used for over 800 years to fix the kinds of economic problems that America faces today. After this, I will explain how tariffs will fix the specific problems outlined in Chapters 1 through 3. Lastly, I will explain how America can use tariffs to grow the economy.

TARIFFS "FOR DUMMIES"

To begin with, a *tariff* is a tax on imported goods. Typically, tariffs are levied according on particular types of goods, or on goods imported from countries. For example, America would be at liberty to raise tariffs on rum but not whisky, or on rum made in Cuba but not from Jamaica. Tariffs have two purposes.

First, the tariff is a tax that raises revenue for the government. Second, and more importantly, tariffs only raise the cost of imported goods—not of goods that are made in America. This makes the cost of imported products more expensive relative to American-made products, thereby nudging consumers to buy American. If they do so, Americans not only support local businesses, but they will also avoid paying the tax entirely. If only it were so easy to get out of paying income tax!

Many so-called conservatives are ideologically opposed to tariffs because they are a form of taxation. We are told that all taxes are bad. No exceptions. While this argument may hold true in an ideal world, we must remember that we do not live in an ideal world. We live in the real world. Things here are messy, to say the least. Just as Plato's idealistic theories failed at Syracuse, so too have America's conservative ideologues failed to enrich America by bulldozing our historic tariff walls and embracing free trade.

Taxes are a tool—albeit a dangerous tool—which are neither good nor bad. Instead, it is how we choose to apply our taxes that causes harm. We should not be afraid to raise tariffs w hen doing so is in our national and economic self interest.

Now that we know what tariffs are, how to they work? Most political commentators wrongly assume that tariffs work like a sales tax. That is, they assume that a 10% tariff on toasters will raise the price of toasters by 10%. This is false. Unlike a sales tax, America's tariffs are not applied to a product's retail price, which is the price consumers pay at the supermarket. Likewise, tariffs are not applied to the wholesale price, which is the bulk price that stores like Walmart pay for goods. In fact, tariffs are not necessarily levied on the entire import price of the product.

Instead, tariffs are levied on the *first sale price*, which is the price American corporations, or their agents, pay to foreign vendors. This method of calculation reduces the cost of tariffs to American consumers, but preserves the punitive effects of tariffs on foreign producers.

For example, imagine America imposes a 10% tariff on all Chinese toasters. Companies like Black & Decker make toasters in China. These toasters sell for $60.00 in American retail stores.[118] Many in the media will claim that this will raise the cost of toasters to $66.00. This is untrue. Tariffs are not raised on a product's retail price—$66.00 toasters are a media-concocted boogeyman.

This begs the question: how much will a 10% tariff raise the cost of toasters for American consumers?

American distributors buy their toasters from Chinese factories. However, because of China's intentionally convoluted regulatory framework, they often use middlemen located in Hong Kong, Singapore, or Taiwan. These middlemen charge the Americans roughly $14.00 for the very same toasters.[119] Of course, the middlemen do not work for free. For their troubles they double the price of the toasters, having bought them from China for $7.00 per toaster.[120]

Given that this is the first sale price, we can estimate that a 10% tariff on Chinese toasters would raise the cost of $60.00 toasters by just 70¢. American consumers do not pay 10% more for toasters—they pay just 1.15% more. And even this assumes that toaster-manufacturers do not simply source the toasters from somewhere other than China.

The same logic applies to the component pieces of manufactured goods. For example, toasters manufactured in Vietnam using Chinese parts will only increase in price relative to the number of Chinese parts they contain. For example, if a Taiwanese factory assembles toasters for $7.00, and half of the parts are made in China, then only half of its value would be subject to tariffs, and a 10% tariff would only raise the retail price of these Taiwanese toasters in America by just over half a percent. It would, however, render manufacturing toasters in China uneconomical.

In this way, America can use tariffs to accomplish important strategic goals. For example, America could impose tariffs on Chinese semiconductors. Although this would have a relatively minimal impact on the price of computers in America, it could make it uneconomical to manufacture semiconductors in China. This could help America diversify its suppliers, and weaken China's economic leverage over America.

The same logic applies to all other strategic goods. Of course, the ultimate goal of tariffs is not to reallocate American's offshored industries from China to less-threatening countries like Vietnam, but to bring them home, and to reignite the torch of economic growth.

ON EXTERNALITIES AND ECONOMIC DAM-BUILDING

Tariffs make imports more expensive. This removes the economic incentive for corporations to move their production abroad, thereby protecting American jobs and industries from the ravages of the offshoring vicious cycle. While this undeniably true, would it not simply be better to lower the cost of America's goods, rather than raise the cost of imports? Yes, in theory. The problem is that this is simply not practical—nor is it in our national interest. Although this sounds counterintuitive, the reasoning is straightforward.

In the long run, the only way to lower the cost of American goods is to invent and deploy new technologies. Unfortunately, the offshoring vicious cycle eats away at America's industry in the short run. In fact, every industry that moves abroad actually decreases the likelihood that an industry-specific technology will be invented or deployed in America. As such, offshoring is a ticking time bomb that requires more urgent measures to correct. Our tools to do this are simply insufficient.

Republicans have suggested that we can make American industries internationally competitive by reducing the cost of doing business in America. For example, we could lower taxes and cut red tape. Although this would certainly help America's economy, it would not be enough. The fact of the matter is that America could usher in a *laissez faire* libertarian economic paradise—no taxes and anything goes—and it would still not be enough to make us competitive with places like China. Why? One word: *externalities*.

Relative to the developing world, America has strict regulations respecting issues such as labor standards or environmental degradation. These standards impose costs on manufacturers—it costs money to give workers lunch-breaks or to treat toxic waste—and these costs are baked into the final price of an American-made product. The costs are internalized. On the other hand, countries like China do not have such robust regulations, and as a result their goods are "cheaper" than American goods. At least on paper.

In reality, there is a cost to society and the environment for lax regulations. However, these costs are not paid by the producer. Instead, these costs are paid for by society at large: they are *externalized*. For example, China's natural environment has been poisoned by all manner of toxic chemicals and pollutants because the government allowed factories to externalize environmental costs in the name of manufacturing "cheap" goods.

Chinese goods are not cheaper than American goods, they simply do not reflect the full cost of making the product. For this reason, America cannot produce goods as cheaply as China—not unless we are willing to destroy our standard of living—not unless we are willing to sacrifice our environment—not unless we are willing to outlaw morality in the name of business and sell our very soul for profit.

No. Reducing the cost of business so as to compete with China on price is simply not desirable. Nor is it possible. Remember, even if America allowed manufacturers to externalize all costs, China's economy is structurally distinct from America's. In America, private corporations dominate the market. Although these corporations are large, and many are owned by the same few investment firms, like Blackrock or Berkshire Hathaway, they remain private entities.

In China, however, all major business entities are arms of the state, and are backed by its monolithic might. As a result, Chinese companies can engage in unprofitable business practices which would ultimately destroy private corporations, until such time as they have secured their market share. Frankly, unless America nationalized all key private industry, we could not compete with China. As a result, the *only* way to protect America's market from asymmetrical competition from countries like China is to price-in these externalities to imports by imposing protective tariffs.

In addition to the problems caused by externalities, I would be remised if I did not note the fairly obvious issues caused by a "race to the bottom". Remember, despite America's outsized global importance, the USA is actually quite small in the grand scheme of things. Consider that there are roughly 330 million Americans. Meanwhile, the world is home to just under 8 billion souls. This means that there are about 23 non-Americans for every American—23 people who probably want your job, and would be willing to work for pennies on the dollar.

If American workers competed in a global job market, with no labor protects, economic gravity would pull our wages down. Why? Wealth is like water: it flows downwards until it finds its resting equilibrium.

In a truly free global market, American businesses would universally offshore to take advantage of cheaper foreign labor costs—either that, or American wages would collapse to the global average. Right now, America has the economic high ground, and tariffs are the dam we need to keep our wealth from flowing downstream into Mexico and China.

A DINNER AT LINDY'S DINER

According to Trip Advisor, Lindy's Deli is a remarkably unremarkable diner in New York City. However, a remarkable observation happened to be made at Lindy's: gossip-loving actors noticed that the longer a Broadway musical ran, the longer it continued to run. For example, a play with five performances statistically had just five more. However, if the play happened to make it to 10 performances, 10 more could be expected.

This is why plays like the *Phantom of the Opera*, which has had over 12,000 performances over the last thirty years, is likely to continue to run thirty years from now. Meanwhile, almost no one has heard of—or will ever hear of—*Lestat*, which had 39 performances in the year 2006. Time measures robustness. The longer something lasts, the longer it continues to last. This heuristic is called the *Lindy Effect*.

The Lindy Effect is not foolproof, but it is helpful in determining what is useful and what is not. For example, if your life depended upon guessing what single piece of technology will still be around in 1,000 years—assuming humanity still exists—what would you say? Computers? Internal combustion engines? These are useful modern technologies. But Lindy can do better.

Knives. Knives have been around for tens of thousands of years, and have proven their utility over in every human society. Knives are robust in the fact of technological change: no matter how advanced we become, the knife will remain indispensable.

The same logic applies to economic tools. For example, all civilizations have adopted some form of currency. Although money takes many forms—from giant stone wheels from the Yap Islands, to electrum coins bearing the portraits of ancient Lydian kings, to ledgers stored in the digital cloud—it serves the same purpose: to store value so as to facilitate economic transactions. Money is a Lindy-compatible invention. So too are tariffs.

Tariff-like taxes on imports have been around since at least the Bronze Age. More importantly, tariffs have been used for the last 800 years by Western monarchs and parliaments to protect industries from overwhelming foreign competition, and to encourage local economic development. Although we could focus on just about any European or East Asian country, we will look specifically at Great Britain. Why?

No other country—with the possible exception of the USA herself—used tariffs more effectively than Great Britain. Likewise, no country has suffered more severe economic consequences after dismantling the tariff walls and embracing free trade. In the next three sections we will learn from Britain's successes and failures.

REMEMBER ME TO ONE WHO LIVES THERE...

Our journey begins in the year 1200 A.D. Europe has awoken from the slumbering Dark Ages. Now is a time of unprecedented technological and economic growth, of intellectual curiosity, and vibrant architectural creativity which was unmatched by any previous civilization. Whereas the Greco-Roman world was powered primarily by slavery, Medieval Europe, or Christendom, was a world of machines.

Christians used windmills, watermills, and treadmills to power machinery that automated all manner of simple tasks, from grinding grain, moving cranes, and fulling cloth. The widespread use of machinery allowed Christendom to accomplish incredible industrial feats. For example, the limestone quarries of Northern France alone produced more stone in 300 years than did Ancient Egypt in 3,000.

The economic heart of Christendom was Flanders, a region located in modern Belgium and France.[x] Flanders was Northern Europe's weaving capital. Raw wool was imported from England, and turned into luxury cloth that was then exported to England, France, and Germany. By 1200 A.D. Flanders had acquired a near-monopoly in luxury textiles. There are two reasons for this.

---

x More properly, there were two economic metropoles in the Medieval Era. Flanders was the economic center of Northern Europe, and Northern Italy—particularly Tuscany—was the beating heart of Southern Europe's economy. Interestingly, the history of both regions largely parallel one another. Both regions were quick to deploy machinery to automate simple tasks. Both were the centers of textile manufacturing. And the Renaissance occurred in both regions approximately simultaneously, and spread from there to the rest of Europe.

First, Flanders produced the best quality fabric at the cheapest price. The reason this was possible is because Flanders had the most and best machinery, or as Adam Smith might have phrased it, Flanders had accumulated the most capital equipment.

This brings us to the second reason: no country could compete with Flanders unless it also accumulated sufficient capital. However, competitors could not afford this capital without first competing with Flanders—or borrowing an impossible sum in an age where credit facilities were largely limited to lords. Essentially, Flanders locked-out foreign competition by producing quality goods at a price that could not be matched.

Most of Christendom happily traded with Flanders—what kind of people could complain about good quality products at reasonable prices? The English. The English Crown resented the fact that Flanders grew rich off of English wool. Would it not be better that England both harvest and manufacture the wool, thereby reaping both England's and Flanders' profits?

King Edward III of England (d.1377) made it a core tenant of his reign to develop an English textile industry. To do this, Edward prohibited imports of Flemish cloth; imposed export duties on raw wool, but not on finished cloth; bribed Flemish machinists to set up shop in England; and he went so far as to wear nothing but English fabric himself so as to set a good example for his people. [121] In short, Edward waged a full-scale trade war against Flanders, and it worked.

Edward's tariffs and other protectionist policies created a domestic market for a domestic textile industry. This allowed English weavers to accumulate the capital they needed to eventually compete with the Flemish on even footing. Consider that England's cloth production rose from just 5,000 bolts of cloth in 1350 to over 80,000 in 1500. [122]

Moreover, these tariffs broke Flanders' textile monopoly. For example, cloth production in Ypres dropped by 60% between 1312 and 1360.[123] Overall, England's protectionist policies helped her secure a share of Christendom's most valuable and technologically advanced industry, and this ultimately set the stage for the Industrial Revolution a few centuries later.

Edward's policies were so successful that they were copied by many subsequent English monarchs. For example, King Henry VII (d. 1509) raised tariffs on wool textiles in 1489 temporarily banned the export of raw wool.[124] His granddaughter, Elizabeth I (d. 1603) sealed the deal by permanently prohibiting the exploration of wool. This marked the shift of economic power from Flanders to England, and by 1650 some 80% of all English exports were textiles.[125]

There are two economic lessons in the story of Medieval England worth heeding. First, tariffs can be used to nurture and protect domestic industry from foreign competition. Although this may be economically "inefficient" on the global level—free trade with Flanders certainly made Christendom as a whole richer—protectionism can be exceedingly efficient at the local level. This is because certain industries are more lucrative than others. In this case, England made more profit by protecting its "inefficient" textile industry than it did by specializing on its comparative advantage on sheering sheep.

Second, what is good globally is not always good locally. Consider that Christendom as a whole benefited from Flanders' cheap, high-quality cloth. England destroyed Flanders' textile industry using tariffs and other aggressive trade policies. Ultimately, this resulted in Christendom buying England's relatively expensive, lower-quality cloth instead. In this case, tariffs made England richer and Christendom poorer. Economists could plausibly make the case that tariffs overall did economic harm, but who cares? The goal of any sovereign state must be to protect its own self interest—not the commonweal of all mankind.

THE PIGGYBACK RIDE TO EL DORADO

As we saw in Chapter 3, England continued to protect its domestic industry from foreign competition. For example, in 1651 the English passed the first *Navigation Act*, which forced goods entering England to be transported on English ships. This accomplished two goals.

First, it protected England's shipbuilding industry, which itself supported a host of other industries like textiles, woodworking, and metallurgy. Consider that between 1660 and 1700 England's textile production doubled, largely due to increased domestic and colonial demand for cloth for sailing ships. [126] Second, England turned itself into the bottleneck through which America's riches flowed. This ensured above-market prices for colonial exports, again enriching England at Christendom's expense.

In 1721 Prime Minister Robert Walpole instituted a coherent trade policy which was explicitly designed to turn England into the world's factory. This was based on Walpole's observation—the same observation made by King Edward III or Queen Elizabeth I before him—that it was far more profitable to sell refined goods than raw goods. It was better to sell cloth than wool, ships than lumber, and swords than iron ingots.

As such, Walpole lowered import duties on raw materials, abolished export duties on manufactured goods, raised tariffs on manufactured goods, created "bounties" to subsidize new industries, and increased quality controls on British manufactured goods to ensure that the nation's exports were second to none. [127] Although this level of government involvement in the economy may seem overbearing, the success of a policy must be measured according to its practical outcomes, not its ideological purity. So, the question remains: did Walpole's protectionist policies make Britain rich?

Yes. Between 1721-30 and 1761-70, Britain's average trade surplus with the American colonies grew from £67,000 to £739,000. [128] Not only did British exports increase, the composition changed. Between 1700 and 1773, raw materials and agricultural products, as a percentage of overall British exports, declined from 13.2% to 8.8%, and the share of wool cloth declined from 47.5% to 26.7%.

Conversely, manufactured goods rose from 8.4% to 27.4% of British exports.[129] This category included things like glassware, metal products (tools, nautical instruments), paper, hats, and cotton cloth.[130] Also, Britain cut its imports of manufactured goods by half during the period, (from 31.7% to 16.9%).[131]

The takeaway is this: England's economy diversified and moved up the value-chain during this period. Rather than being a nation of shepherds, Great Britain became a nation of mechanics and merchants. In fact, by the time of the American Revolution, some 18.5% of Britain's male population was already employed in the manufacturing sector.[132]

This was possible because of Walpole's protectionist trade policies, which guaranteed British manufactures access to a much larger domestic and colonial market than they would have had under a free trade regime. This allowed Great Britain to not only accumulate more capital equipment, but to produce more technologically sophisticated goods. These conditions set the stage for the Industrial Revolution, which ushered in a new age of nearly-infinite material prosperity.

ON THE INDUSTRIAL REVOLUTION AND ITS CAUSES

The Nineteenth Century witnessed the apotheosis of Great Britain as the richest and most technologically advanced economy in human history. This was caused by the *Industrial Revolution*, the period in which mankind invented a way to harvest virtually unlimited energy from coal to mass produce consumer goods.

The Industrial Revolution started in Great Britain in the 1760s and continued in earnest until the 1840s, before spreading throughout the West. Even today, the main difference between First World and Third World countries is whether or not said country has industrialized—and yes, large portion of the globe remain incapable of industrializing even to this day. Before I show you how the Industrial Revolution perfectly exemplifies the model of economic growth proposed in Chapter 8 of this book, I need you to "unlearn" most of what you "know" about the Industrial Revolution, because it is probably very wrong.

Most Americans are taught in school that the Industrial Revolution was fueled by two factors. First, Britain's urban population rapidly expanded because of the advent of crop rotation, and the *Enclosure Acts* which forced peasants off of the land. Second, Britain adopted laissez faire capitalism domestically and free trade internationally, which expanded the market for British goods. Both of these alleged causes are entirely backwards. The Industrial Revolution occurred at a time when Great Britain was suffering from an acute labor shortage, and when the Island was economically isolated both by high tariffs and foreign embargoes.

Great Britain was one of Europe's smallest powers. Its population of 5.7 million people was dwarfed by that of its two main rivals, France, with 25 million people, and Spain, with 8.4 million people. In fact, Great Britain was not even three times as large as the American Colonies.

Despite this demographic disadvantage, Great Britain was constantly at war with its much larger neighbors, which include major conflicts like such as the Seven Year's War (1756 – 1763), fought against France, Spain, the Holy Roman Empire, Russia, and Sweden; the American Revolutionary War (1775 – 1783) fought against the Thirteen Colonies, France, Spain, and the Netherlands; and the Wars of the French Revolution and Napoleonic Wars (1793 – 1815), fought against every European power save Portugal.

On top of this, Britain imposed the highest tariffs in all of Europe, and continued to raise them throughout this period. For example, average tariff rates climbed from 30% in the 1700s up to 57% in the early 1820s.[133]

In order to survive these conflicts, Great Britain needed to produce as much war materiel as its rivals, all the while fielding similar numbers of soldiers and sailors. For example, in the Battle of Trafalgar (1805) the Royal Navy pitted 33 warships against 18 from France and 15 from Spain—Britain deployed more ships despite being one quarter the size of its rivals. Further, Great Britain was far more militarized than was France during the Napoleonic Wars, which further strained her economy.

Consider that Napoleon's *Grande Armée* consisted of 550,000 men. Meanwhile Britain enlisted 250,000 men by land and another 120,000 by sea, and her fleet was as large as the rest of the world's combined. In total, roughly 8.3% of Britain's male population served in the Napoleonic Wars, compared with just 4.5% of France's.[134] This demographic strain, combined with the inability to import manufactured goods from Europe, created enormous economic *necessity*—and as we saw in Chapter 8, necessity is the mother of invention.

If you will recall, necessity alone will not cause long run economic growth. The economy also needs access to a population with sufficient *intelligence*, the right *personality*, and enough *knowledge*. Great Britain had that in spades.

In terms of intelligence, Dutton and Charlton's research has demonstrated that England's average IQ likely peaked immediately preceding the Industrial Revolution, and has been decreasing slowly ever since. This conclusion is based upon the fact that prior to the Industrial Revolution, mortality was *eugenic*, in the sense that the offspring of wealthy men much more likely to survive than were the offspring of poor men. Given the strong correlation between economic success and IQ—a correlation which remains true to this day—Dutton and Charlton surmise that IQs were gradually increasing in England for centuries.

This paradigm shifted during the Industrial Revolution, when Britain's economic elite and intelligentsia began having fewer children, and infant mortality numbers among Britain's poor decreased. At this point, breeding became somewhat *dysgenic*, and the average IQ of Great Britain has actually been decreasing since the Victorian Age.

This is confirmed by the work of Francis Galton, Charles Darwin's half-cousin, who assiduously documented the increase in average reaction times among people in the late Nineteenth Century. As reaction time is highly correlated with IQ, Dutton and Charlton reasonably conclude that IQ has been decreasing ever since mankind industrialized.

In any case, Great Britain was home to a highly intelligent population—a population which was likely much more intelligent than it is today. The next factor, a population with a favorable balance between social and asocial personalities, cannot be quantified based on the historical data. That said, the fact that Great Britain produced so many geniuses during this period makes it self-evident that there were enough people with *endogenous personalities* to facilitate invention.

Lastly, Great Britain's population had enough *knowledge* to facilitate the Industrial Revolution. Remember, knowledge does not necessarily refer to formal education—nor does it necessarily refer to basics such as literacy or numeracy. Instead, a knowledgeable population is one which both theoretically understands, and has practical experience with, the most advanced technologies of the day. Because of Walpole's protectionism, many more Britons worked with machinery than would have organically. As such, the British population was acquainted with machinery to a degree not found anywhere else in contemporary Europe—save for perhaps the Netherlands.

All of the factors mentioned in Chapter 8 came together during the Industrial Revolution, which was ultimately a product of technological growth. For example, James Watt's steam engine, which was invented some time around

1775, was both twice as powerful as alternative steam engines, and provided rotary power, which was useful for industrial applications. The steam engine liberated machinery from watermills by providing a portable source of power.

The steam engine also opened the door for other important inventions, such as Edmund Cartwright's power loom, invented in 1784, which made British textile workers 40 times as productive as their European competitors. [135] Technologies like the steam engine and the power loom turned Great Britain into the "factory of the world", and enriched Great Britain—and all of humanity—to this day.

Not only did the steam engine greatly increase economic productivity in its own right, but it also fueled further technological development. It did this in two ways. First, the steam engine greatly improved worker productivity by automating simple tasks. This freed workers—particularly skilled artisans like smiths—from wasting their time on repetitive manual tasks. Instead, they were able to delegate these tasks to machines or less-skilled workers, while they focused on tinkering with their new technology, or dreaming up new applications for said technology.

Second, as more Britons were exposed to the technology, more people thought of creative ways to apply the technology. For example, steam engines were adapted to drive pumps in mines, power all manner of machine tools, and drive locomotives. Further, many of these important inventions were created by people with limited formal education. George Stephenson, for example, was a former mineworker and engine-wright who built the steam engine for the world's first public railway.

The Industrial Revolution is also a perfect example of how economic growth is path dependent. There are two points worth mentioning. First, technology builds on what came before: steamships and steam locomotives for railways could only be invented after the steam engine, not earlier. As such, only places which quickly adopted steam engines were in a position to invent or adopt the technologies derived from steam engines. This explains why Great Britain, and places closely connected to Britain either geographically or culturally, has been the epicenter of technological and economic growth for the last two centuries.

Second, people invest their money in industries where they expect to make the greatest returns on their investment. Meanwhile, industries with greater investment tend to generate higher returns simply because they can use said investment to accumulate more capital or take bigger risks. Together, these factors form a positive feedback loop: lucrative industries attract investment, and investment makes industries more lucrative.

Great Britain benefited enormously from increased investment during the Industrial Revolution. Consider that in 1700 just 4% of British national income was reinvested. The vast majority of income was spent on consumption. However, by 1800 this number had doubled to 8.5%. By 1840 a maximum of 10.8% of British national income was reinvested.[136] This was important because it allowed British industries to accumulate more capital and spend more money on research, which further fueled economic growth.

SHYLOCK'S REVENGE

Perhaps more instructive than how Great Britain succeeded is how it failed.

Britain was the supreme political and economic power of the early nineteenth century. Not only had her victory in the Napoleonic Wars guaranteed her place as the World's military hegemon, but her Empire continued to grow beyond comprehension. Britain eventually ruled one quarter of the world. Hers was a realm of perpetual daylight. Likewise, her economy was unmatched: the Industrial Revolution brought with it the sort of prosperity never before seen by the likes of men. She was the factory of the world: if something existed, Britain made it.

It was not until the middle of the century that things began to change. Britain's parliament was consumed by debates over the merits of a radical new ideology: *free trade*. Politicians speculated and deliberated, insults were exchanged, but ultimately free trade became Britain's credo—after all, it looked good on paper. The tariff wall that had protected British industry since the Middle Ages was quickly dismantled from highs of over 50% in the 1820s, to just 5% decades later.[137] Britain became history's first and only major free-trading nation.

Great Britain's politicians likewise managed to convince many of its European neighbors to embrace international free trade. Tariffs were reduced to some of their lowest levels in history by the middle of the Nineteenth Century. Great Britain's industries benefited enormously, as their inexpensive, high quality manufactured goods stormed Europe's markets—just as how inexpensive, high quality Flemish cloth had once saturated England's textile market.

The effects on Europe were predictable. European industries lost market share, and economic growth slowed to a craw. In fact, Europe's weakest average economic and industrial growth of the Nineteenth Century, 1.7% and 1.8% respectively, coincided with this free trade experiment.[138]

It did not take long for European governments to protect their failing industries from Great Britain's more productive factories. During the 1870s most European nations rebuilt their tariff walls, and "copied" Prime Minister Robert Walpole's playbook from the previous century. These strategies worked. Between 1891 and 1911 GNP growth in continental Europe averaged 2.6%, while industrial output grew at 3.8%— over twice as fast as during the liberal era.[139]

Great Britain, foolishly, stuck to its guns and doubled down on free trade. After all, the experts had "proven" that free trade worked on paper. What happened next mirrors what has been happening to America since 1973. Great Britain's manufacturing supremacy eroded. British factories were forced to compete with European factories, which were often propped-up by their governments—much as how American factories "compete" with Chinese state-backed factories today. It was not a fair fight.

Great Britain's exports fell, and imports rose, and the nation ushered in a new era of chronic trade deficits. Between 1873 and 1883 the value of British exports actually fell by 6%—the days of endless growth were over.[140] This led to a full-blown "made in Germany" crisis. Britain even found itself importing steel from Spain, for the first time since the Middle Ages when Spanish swords were in vogue.[141]

In the late Victorian Age Britain's economic growth stagnated, and was 55% slower than it was during the middle of the century.[142] Slowing growth was caused by a sluggish manufacturing sector, which was forced to compete for market share with government-backed foreign rivals. Between 1870 and 1913 British manufacturing grew by only 2.1% on average, whereas German manufacturing grew by 4.7% on average.[143]

Adding to this problem was the fact that British investors chased higher returns abroad, rather than reinvesting their profits in Britain. Consider this: in 1815, the British invested only £10 million abroad, but by 1825 this had increased to £100 million, and by 1870 over £700 million left the country.[144] By 1914, fully 35% of British wealth was held abroad.[xi] Northern Britain became a rustbelt. Once great cities like Glasgow and Manchester became the "Detroits" of their age.

By the outbreak of the First World War, Britain was merely a first among equals, as opposed the unrivaled superpower she had been a half-century earlier. This was Britain's fate, and America's will be no different. The same arrogance

---

xi Davis & Gallman, *Evolving Financial Markets and International Capital Flows*, 58. True, some of this increase was because Britain was getting richer, and had more money to spend abroad. However, by the 1870s, domestic investment actually started falling (even as it picked up steam abroad). See: Chambers, *The Workshop of the World: British Economic history from 1820-1880*, 89.

afflicts us, while global free trade eats away at our prosperity like an incurable infection.

It is funny though, the similarities as to why both countries adopted free trade. Sure, some genuinely believed it was a panacea, but others were more Machiavellian. For example, Lord Goderich said of Britain's free trade policy that:

> *other nations knew... that what we meant by free trade, was nothing*
> *more nor less than, by means of the great advantages we enjoyed, to get*
> *the monopoly of all their markets for our manufactures, and to prevent*
> *them, one and all, from ever becoming manufacturing nations.* [145]

Lord Goderich recognized that many British politicians thought they could weaponize free trade in order to lock their rivals into a lower level of economic development. Perhaps this strategy would have worked had these nations played by Britain's rules—as did Britain's loyal colonies. But they did not, and the rest is history.

Great Britain did not adopt free trade for purely economic reasons, and neither did America. We became a bastion of free trade in part to differentiate ourselves from the USSR. Free trade was as much about propaganda as it was about economics. The Soviet Union is dead, and America is dying. It is time to go back to what worked. It is time for America to again embrace American School economics and rebuild the tariff walls that helped to make America rich in the first place.

DEFENDING THE AMERICAN SYSTEM

Our Founding Fathers built a tariff wall around this great nation. They did this for three main reasons. First, tariffs were one of the least-intrusive forms of taxation that they could think of. Why? Tariffs are a completely avoidable tax—if you do not want to pay tax, then buy American. Simple.

Second, the tariffs protected America's nascent industries from unfair foreign competition, and therefore ensured that America not only industrialized, but would grow economically self-sufficient. After all, a country that cannot manufacture its own tools and weapons will not long remain free. Third, the Founding Fathers observed that tariffs had made Great Britain rich at the Colonies' expense—if they worked in Britain they would work in America. The Founding Fathers respected the wisdom of history, and tariffs were simply a time-tested strategy that had proven their effectiveness. Why reinvent the wheel?

If tariffs made America rich once, they could do it again. I will explain how, but first, I will explain how tariffs can be used to fix America's economic malaise. In Chapters 1 through 3 we surveyed some of the biggest economic problems plaguing American citizens. We saw how millions of Americans have lost their jobs and dropped out of the labor force entirely. Not only are over 12 million Americans unemployed, but at least 8 million more can only find part time jobs.

We also witnessed that the American Dream of owning a home and raising a big, beautiful family on a single income is now almost impossible. Young Americans are increasingly locked out of the housing market, because houses now cost 95% more, in real terms, than they did in 1973. Likewise, most American workers actually earn *less* than they did in 1973.

To add insult to injury, America's industries are hollowed-out. At this point, America's economy is so emasculated that are forced to hitch rides on Russian rockets to reach own our space station. Further, we are almost entirely dependent upon our greatest rival nation, China, for the necessities of life. If trade relations were to break down, America's economy would be on the verge of collapse within months. Why? We do not manufacture nearly enough machine tools or silicon chips to maintain our own economy. The sword of Damocles hangs above us, suspended by a single thread, while we remain blithely unaware of our impending collapse.

In Chapter 4 we explored how international trade works. We learned that America has ran a trade deficit every year since 1973, meaning that we have bought more than we sold to the world. Of course, there is no such thing as a free lunch: America paid for this trade deficit by selling our assets, like ownership of our land and corporations, and promising to pay in the future, by borrowing large amounts of debt.

We witnessed some of the consequences of this Faustian bargain. For example, foreign buyers have driven-up the cost of housing dramatically. Meanwhile, Americans have borrowed enormous sums of money to try and keep up with inflation. All of this is to say that America is poorer today than it was yesterday.

This poverty has caused all sorts of non-economic harms. For example, chronic unemployment and underemployment has led to the rise of various asocial "escapist" behaviors. This has contributed to the rise in drug use—particularly opioids in the Midwest—which kills 70,000 people every year.

On top of this, America's decreased purchasing power has led Americans to swap healthy animal fats for poisonous and undigestible seed oils. This has made Americans unhealthy by increasing their rates of obesity, diabetes, and cancer, decreasing America's testosterone levels, and impeding the functioning of our immune systems. In short, the trade deficit is not only impoverishing us, it is *killing* us.

Thankfully, tariffs can fix these problems. How?

These problems are caused by the trade deficit and the offshoring vicious cycle. Tariffs will break this cycle by raising the cost of imports so high that companies have no choice but to move their production back to America. As we saw in Chapter 5, this could relocate between 6.2 and 11.7 million jobs back to America—jobs which our consumption currently supports in places like Canada, Mexico, and China. This would be the first step in rebuilding America's shattered economy.

Various Chicken Littles in the media contend that tariffs will not bring these jobs home, and instead corporations will simply abandon the American market. This is completely asinine. Although this argument may hold true for small countries like Haiti, America is the largest consumer market in the world, and it would be profitable for all businesses to either reopen their American factories or at the very least build satellite factories to service the American market. Do not fear, tariffs will not prevent you from buying the latest iPhone, they will simply ensure that it is both designed *and manufactured* in California. Win-win.

Other talking heads have argued that tariffs will raise the cost of consumer goods. This is true, but only in the short term. Tariffs will increase the cost of goods which are not made in America. This will increase the cost of most goods, because most goods are not made in America. *Ipso facto*, consumer prices will increase. However, this will not always be the case. Once America again manufactures everything that the consumer market demands, the prices will actually *decrease*. Why? Three reasons.

First, the price differential between manufacturing in America and China is not nearly as large as you would expect. In fact, a gadget that costs $1.00 to manufacture in America costs $0.96 to manufacture in China.[146] This is because of a phenomenon called the Law of Increasing Returns, which states that the per-unit cost of a mass-produced good *decreases* with each additional unit produced.

Frankly, I doubt whether most consumers would notice a 4% increase in prices on consumer goods—the difference between a case of plastic forks that costs $22.99 and $23.99 is imperceptible, it is a rounding error. In any case, the government could quite easily slash sales tax in conjunction with the increase in tariffs, and zero-out this increase in prices altogether.

Second, consumer goods will decrease in price in the long run whether or not they are made in China or America. This is because price is a function of productivity, and continued productivity improvements eventually reduce the price of all goods to almost nothing. Given a long enough time horizon, you will find that when you graph the price of consumer goods the graph will approximate a horizontal asymptote.

This is because goods are at their most expensive when they are first invented—this is the point where they likely have the most relative utility and are the most difficult to produce—and they become cheap once their utility becomes ubiquitous and their production is optimized. For example, the first computers were hulking beasts that filled entire rooms and cost millions of dollars. Today, computers are so ubiquitous and cheap that they are often given away as promotional gifts.[147] The same is true of most consumer goods from knives to telephones.

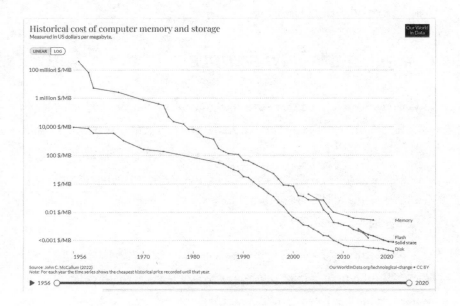

Third, in Chapter 3 worker productivity and wages rose in lockstep prior to 1973. During this period wages rose faster than inflation, and people were able to spend more on wants than needs. Global free trade decoupled this relationship by opening what was essentially a closed system.

Tariffs will help to close the economic system again and restore the nexus between work and earnings. This will decrease the cost of not only consumer goods, but houses too—the prices of which will likewise fall because fewer foreign buyers will compete with America for our real estate. History shows us that tariffs can put this genie back in the lamp.

Finally, tariffs will help America to reindustrialize. I will not belabor this point. Tariffs will make imports more expensive than American goods. As such, investors will open factories to produce everything that America needs. This will make our nation economically self-sufficient, just as the founders intended.

Further, because of the logic of the Law of Increasing Returns, it is likely that American factories would be coopted to service foreign markets as well. Essentially, tariffs will leverage the power and size of America's consumer market to rebuild our industrial production.

RUMPELSTILTSKIN'S SPINDLE

In Chapter 8 we learned that economic growth is a function of technological growth. Unfortunately, we cannot force people to invent new paradigm-shifting technologies. They are *black swan* events which are highly improbably yet highly consequential. Nevertheless, we are able to identify a number of factors that increase the likelihood of these black swan events. To begin with, *necessity* is the mother of invention.

Next, it helps if the economy has an *intelligent* and *knowledgeable* population with the right mix of *endogenous personalities*. Also, in order to thrive, people need to be *free* to identify problems, and to dream and deploy creative solutions. Lastly—and perhaps most obviously—economies that are both *big* and *diverse* are more likely to breed black swans. Tariffs will improve America, either directly or indirectly, across every metric.

Tariffs can create economic necessity by making imports prohibitively expensive. This forces the local economy to pick up the slack to fill in the economic gaps. This conclusion is not based on mere navel-gazing, as are so many economic theories, but is supported by the preponderance of historical evidence.

For example, when King Edward III prohibited imports of Flemish cloth, Englishmen responded by building new textile mills to clothe king and country. This likewise occurred at the dawn of the Industrial Revolution, wherein the British people were forced to make more with less, due to the Island's economic isolation. Finally, America's Founding Fathers used tariffs to make it impossible for our nation to depend upon Europe for its economic livelihood—tariffs forced America to industrialize and prosper, or languish as a colonial backwater.

As we have discussed previously, the economy is a complex system. One of the peculiar features of complex systems is that they often behave organically. For example, complex systems as differentiated and unique as conifer forests, the human body, and the economy all respond to non-lethal perturbances or stressors by growing stronger.

Consider the conifer forests which belt the northern hemisphere. Every year there are thousands of forest fires which reduces swathes of the forest to blackened ash. The billowing smoke can be seen from space, often settling hundreds of miles away as a thin layer of ash. Although these fires may eradicate an individual copse, they replenish the soil with nutrients and create space for new growth. The systemic stress caused by fires rejuvenate the forest, strengthening its flora and fauna in the long run.

The same is true of the human body. The world's first bodybuilder and strongman, Milo of Croton, built his Herculean physique by carrying a calf on his back every day. As the calf fattened, so too did Milo's sinews and tendon thicken. This logic also applies to the economy.

The economy benefits from stressors—non-existential wars, trade embargoes and tariffs, or strenuous free market competition—which winnow away the chaff until only the wheat remains. Tariffs will stress the economy by making imports expensive. This will force the economy to strengthen and to adapt. Likewise, tariffs will increase competition by allowing for the creation of American businesses, which have been priced out of the international market by unquantified externalities.

The next ingredient for economic growth is the right kind of people. Although tariffs will not raise America's IQ or change our collective personality, they will help to make Americans more knowledgeable. Further, they will ensure the economy provides more opportunities for our best and brightest. Remember, knowledge refers to both theoretical understanding and practical experience with technology. Although Americans have ample theoretical knowledge, offshoring has greatly reduced the number of people with practical experience with various technologies.

Tariffs will re-shore America's industry and necessitate this knowledge acquisition. This will benefit America similar to how the proliferation of the steam engine benefited Britain—people who otherwise would not have been exposed to technology will learn how it works, and can put their minds to work. Remember, most inventors are not Caltech or Harvard alumni, instead they are often mechanics and tinkerers who invented better ways of doing things to make their own jobs easier. The more Americans work with advanced technology, the better.

Next, tariffs will make America freer. My detractors will claim this is impossible: tariffs are a tax, and taxation is theft! To this, I have two responses.

232

First, tariffs will create jobs and increase the purchasing power of ordinary Americans. This will help to rebuild America's once affluent middle class, which safeguarded America's freedoms in a way that America's working poor cannot. Personal independence—like political independence—rests upon financial independence. It is simply a fact that someone who has "fuck you" money is more likely to choose their principles over an unnecessary paycheck. Likewise, people with savings are much more likely start businesses and eventually become self-employed.

Second, tariffs will increase economic freedom by increasing competition. As we have noted, sheltering local American businesses from asymmetrical and unfair Chinese competition will provide opportunities for local businesses to grow. Further, this will reduce the power of multinational corporations, who use their factories in China to out-compete local American businesses—who often produce better quality products to begin with. Tariffs level the playing field so that more Americans can actually compete in the economy.

Finally, tariffs will increase the size and diversity of America's economy, making it more likely that new technology will be invented in America. The logic underpinning this is straightforward.

First, sufficiently high tariffs will eliminate the trade deficit and force American businesses to increase their production to make our consumption. This will grow the economy and create millions of jobs. Given that the size of the economy is correlated with the rate of invention, a bigger economy cannot be a bad thing. Further, tariffs will increase America's economic diversity by requiring America to produce everything it requires, rather than filling in the gaps with imports.

Tariffs will increase the likelihood of technological, and therefore economic, growth by boosting most of the contributing factors. However, the most important way that they will grow the economy is by protecting the lead that we already have.

In Chapter 8 we learned that technological growth is path dependent. This means that new technologies can only be invented in places where the newest technologies were themselves recently invented or adopted. This explains why almost all consequential technologies were either invented in Western Europe or America—these regions were first to industrialize, and have simply been carried forward into the future by their own inertia. This is supported by the work of Lynn and Vanhannen, who found that Europe's industrial heartland has remained richer than one could predict given the best available metrics.

Although America's economy is badly bruised, the nation still leads the world in technological development. These technologically advanced industries are the engine of economic growth, and they are frighteningly in the process of offshoring to places like China, Germany, and Mexico. This must be stopped at all costs.

America cannot—must not—blunt our cutting edge with offshoring. Doing so would demolish the prosperity that took our ancestors two and a half centuries to accumulate, and end forever the American Dream.

EPILOGUE

There was a time when people from the Old World clamored on ships and braved the icy Atlantic to come to America. Their dream was our dream, the American Dream—to pursue wealth and happiness. The raise a family. To serve God. To build a life worth living. For centuries our ancestors delivered on this promise. Out of many peoples grew one nation under God. America was a light to the world.

The American Dream is dying. Today, our economy is growing slower than it was even during the Great Depression. Meanwhile, millions of Americans have lost their jobs. Millions more work part time, scrounging dollars and pinching pennies to make rent. Those Americans who were lucky enough to keep their jobs have seen their earnings stagnate relative to inflation. In fact, wages have not risen for most people since 1973. As such, Americans spend more on rent and groceries than they have since Ronald Reagan was president.

To make matters worse, the American nation has been economically neutered. At one time America was the world's factory. Now, America cannot even manufacture enough machine tools or silicon computer chips to sustain our economy. We are at China's mercy.

In this book we not only surveyed the economic damage, but we uncovered the deeper reasons why the economy was collapsing. America's production is moving to foreign countries like China and Mexico, and importing it back in exchange for our past and future. America's trade deficit costs our nation over $800 *billion* every year, and this number is growing. We also connected the dots, and found that the trade deficit cuts to the heart of America's problems—and not just our economic problems, but our social problems as well.

We saw how mass unemployment and increasing poverty has fed the beast of divorce, pornography addiction, and substance abuse. Free trade is killing America in a literal sense. Moreover, we saw how our declining purchasing power is making us sick. When people cannot afford to eat healthy, they make dietary substitutions. For example, many Americans switched from butter to seed oil. This has caused a precipitous rise in obesity, diabetes, and cancer rates. It has also emasculated our men by reducing testosterone levels, generation after generation.

We then investigated the claims of the dismal science, and found that modern economics is based on false presumptions. This calls into question everything that economists say is true. We looked at the arguments in favor of free trade, and found that they were not only weak, they were absurd. After this, we explored the arguments of other thinkers, and saw that they cannot explain how economic growth works. We then discovered that economic growth is a product of technological growth—economists have been asking the wrong question for centuries.

Lastly, we saw that tariffs can be used to fix America's economy problems, and to grow the economy. Although this is the exact opposite of what economists tell us to do, the logic and evidence is irrefutable. America does not benefit from "free trade" with the likes of China or Mexico—nor even Canada or Great Britain. It is time for Americans to once again put America first, and rebuild the tariff walls. I will conclude as I began, by paying homage to my spiritual predecessor, Thomas Paine:

> On these grounds I rest the matter. WHEREFORE, instead of gazing at each other with suspicious or doubtful curiosity, let each of us hold out to his neighbor the hearty hand of friendship, and unite in drawing a line, which, like an act of oblivion, shall bury in forgetfulness every former dissention. Let the names of [Democrat] and [Republican] be extinct; and let none other be heard among us, than those of a good citizen; an open and resolute friend; and a virtuous supporter of the RIGHTS of MANKIND, and of the FREE AND INDEPENDANT STATES OF AMERICA.

ENDNOTES

Ibid., p. 214.

Ridley, Palmerston, p. 292.

1 Speech of President Clinton via The American Presidency Project. (https://www.presidency. ucsb.edu/)

2 Workopolis. "Only 2% of Applicants Actually Get Interviews" (https://careers.workopolis.com/ advice/only-2-of-applicants-actually-get-interviews-heres-how-to-be-one-of-them/)

3 BLS News Release dated October 4, 2019. (https://www.bls.gov/news.release/archives/ empsit_10042019.pdf)

4 Ellison, Katherine. "American Workers Feel Overqualified, But Aren't Ready to Stop Learning." (https://www.businesswire.com/news/home/20110531005230/en/American-Workers-Feel-Overqualified-But-Aren%E2%80%99t-Ready-to-Stop-Learning)

5 Rose, Stephen J. "Mismatch". (https://www.urban.org/sites/default/files/publication/87951/ college_mismatch_final_2.pdf)

6 Hipple, "People Who Are Not in the Labor Force: Why Aren't they Working?" Footnote 3.

7 Social Security Administration. "Selected Data from Social Security's Disability Program."

8 https://www.pewresearch.org/fact-tank/2018/09/24/stay-at-home-moms-and-dads-account-for-about-one-in-five-u-s-parents/ & https://www.pewresearch.org/social-trends/2014/04/08/after-decades-of-decline-a-rise-in-stay-at-home-mothers/

9 Ibid. 5.

10 Ibid. 6.

11 Gould, "State of Working America Wages 2019." (https://www.epi.org/publication/swa-wages-2019/#:~:text=The%20median%20wage%20in%202019,gaps%20by%20gender%20and%20race.)

12 Chao, "100 Years of US Consumer Spending, Data for the Nation, New York City, and Boston." & BLS data. (https://www.bls.gov/opub/100-years-of-u-s-consumer-spending.pdf)

13 https://burgerlad.com/mcdonald-usa-menu-prices/

14 Prices taken from. https://www.thepeoplehistory.com/70selectrical.html Inflation data from BLS

15 https://www.cnet.com/home/kitchen-and-household/how-to-buy-a-washing-machine/

16 https://www.angi.com/articles/how-much-does-dishwasher-cost.htm

17 https://www.searshomeservices.com/blog/how-long-do-appliances-usually-last

18 https://www.dispatch.com/content/stories/home_and_garden/2014/08/03/fancy--fragile.html

19 https://nationaleconomicseditorial.com/2017/05/12/household-appliances-cheaper-historically/

20 https://www.stuff.co.nz/business/69703891/lifespans-of-household-whiteware-take-a-tumble

21 Ammous, Saifedean. The Fiat Standard. (2021). P. 141

22 https://fred.stlouisfed.org/series/MSPUS

23 https://fred.stlouisfed.org/series/CUSR0000SEHA

24 https://www.youtube.com/watch?v=G-J86Ka9MkQ

25 Ibid. 76.

26 Shepherd and Walton, *Shipping, Maritime Trade and the Economic Development of Colonial North America.* 42.

27 Shepherd & Walton, *The Economics of Early America,* 68.

28 Ibid.

29 Tucker & Tucker, *Industrializing Antebellum America,* 95.

30 Shepherd & Walton, *The Economics of Early America,* 197.

31 United States Congress, *United States Statutes At Large, Vol 1,* 24. This was, in fact, America's second ever piece of legislation.

32 Northrup, Cynthia Clark. *The American Economy,* 2008, p. 233.

33 Hamilton, "Report on Manufactures," 314, 317.

34 Washington, "First Annual Message to Congress on the State of the Union, January 8, 1790."

35 Jefferson, "Letter to Benjamin Austin, Jan 9, 1816."

36 Lincoln as quoted in: Richard Lawrence Miller, *Lincoln and His World.*

37 Curtiss, *Industrial Development of Nations Vol 3,* 6.

38 Grant as quoted in: A.G. Frank, *Capitalism and Underdevelopment in Latin America,* 164.

39 Roosevelt, Theodore. "State of the Union 1902."

40 https://mappinghistory.uoregon.edu/english/US/US26-02.html

41 https://globalupside.com/top-10-manufacturing-countries-in-the-world/

42 https://www.cdc.gov/drugoverdose/epidemic/index.html

43 Scott, "China, Trade, Outsourcing and Jobs," 18. (https://www.epi.org/publication/china-trade-outsourcing-and-jobs/)

44 Bivens & Mishel, "Understanding the Historic Divergence Between Productivity and a Typical Worker's Pay" 3. (https://www.epi.org/publication/understanding-the-historic-divergence-between-productivity-and-a-typical-workers-pay-why-it-matters-and-why-its-real/)

45 https://www.thoughtco.com/henry-ford-and-the-assembly-line-1779201

46 *Gorillawire "40 Surprising Products That Are No Longer Made in America."*

47 Poe, "Lenovo cranks up Whitsett Plant." & Mack, "Are Any Smartphones Not Made in China?"

48 https://www.statista.com/statistics/264213/leading-countries-in-machine-tool-production-based-on-market-share/

49 The precise metric used has two components that both must be satisfied: the industry must spend in the top quintile in R&D and >21% of its workforce must have advanced skills/education in STEM fields. See Muro et al. "America's Advanced Industries: What they are, where they are, and why they matter," 2.

50 Ibid. 6.

51 Ibid. 7.

52 Selvaggio, "Outsourcing Statistics: The Pros and Cons."

53 https://oec.world/en/visualize/tree_map/hs92/export/usa/chn/show/2021

54 Muro et al. "America's Advanced Industries: What they are, where they are, and why they matter," 32.

55 https://www.forbes.com/sites/stevehanke/2018/12/18/president-trumps-trade-rubbish/?sh=dfe91803eaac

56 https://www.law.nyu.edu/sites/default/files/Who%E2%80%99s%20Left%20to%20 Tax%3F%20US%20Taxation%20of%20Corporations%20and%20Their%20Shareholders-%20 Rosenthal%20and%20Burke.pdf & Jackson "Foreign Ownership of US financial assets: implications of a withdrawal." 1.

57 https://www.cnbc.com/2021/11/05/real-estate-brokers-brace-for-flood-of-wealthy-buyers-from-overseas-.html

58 https://sgp.fas.org/crs/misc/RS22331.pdf

59 Bureau of Economic Analysis. "UN Net International Investment Position, First Quarter 2016."

60 Doyle, C. *A Study in Scarlet.*

61 Doyle, C. *A Study in Scarlet.*

62 Doyle, C. "The Adventure of the Cardboard Box".

63 Doyle, C. "The blanched Soldier".

64 Of course, this work both ways. If America had a trade surplus, this would mean that countries offshored production to the US. This is why we must look at the balance of trade, not the overall number of imports, since we also benefit from offshoring (to a lesser degree).

65 Nosbuch & Bernaden. "The Multiplier Effect," 7. & Manufacturing Institute. "Manufacturing's Multiplier Effect is Stronger than Other Sectors'." which says it is 1.33.

66 Scott, "China, Trade, Outsourcing and Jobs," 18.

67 Doyle, C. "The Beryl Coronet".

68 Burke, Edmund. *Reflections on the Revolution in France.* (1790) P.39.

69 Marx, Karl. Speech appended to *The Poverty of Philosophy.* (1885)

70 https://data.oecd.org/youthinac/youth-not-in-employment-education-or-training-neet.htm

71 https://www.forbes.com/sites/jackmccullough/2019/12/09/the-psychopathic-ceo/?sh=c60f368791e3

72 https://www.webmd.com/healthy-aging/news/20051020/early-retirement-early-death

73 https://www.cdc.gov/nchs/products/databriefs/db377.htm

74 https://www.cdc.gov/nchs/products/databriefs/db369.htm

75 https://www.cdc.gov/drugoverdose/epidemic/index.html

76 https://www.therecoveryvillage.com/process-addiction/porn-addiction/pornography-statistics/

77 https://www.jstor.org/stable/26372609

78 https://www.nytimes.com/2018/07/05/upshot/americans-are-having-fewer-babies-they-told-us-why.html#:~:text=Wanting%20more%20leisure%20time%20and,for%20The%20New%20York%20Times.

79 https://www.ncbi.nlm.nih.gov/pmc/articles/PMC4240051/

80 https://docs.iza.org/dp3380.pdf

81 https://downloads.frc.org/EF/EF12C20.pdf

82 https://nationaleconomicseditorial.com/2017/09/20/case-against-economic-globalization/

83 https://allthingsliberty.com/2013/09/the-gunpowder-shortage/

84 http://old.seattletimes.com/html/businesstechnology/2020275838_boeingoutsourcingxml.html

85 https://static1.squarespace.com/static/54ff9c5ce4b0a53decccfb4c/t/59244eed17bffc0ac256 cf16/1495551740633/CarbonPricing_Final_May29.pdf

86 https://eos.org/articles/a-dip-in-atmospheric-carbon-may-have-facilitated-dinosaur-dispersal

87   https://data.worldbank.org/indicator/EN.ATM.CO2E.PP.GD

88 http://www.pnas.org/cgi/doi/10.1073/pnas.1006388108

89 https://pubmed.ncbi.nlm.nih.gov/33395930/

90 https://ourworldindata.org/ocean-plastics

91 https://academic.oup.com/jnci/article/93/11/824/2906147

92 https://academic.oup.com/humupd/article/23/6/646/4035689

93 https://academic.oup.com/jcem/article/92/1/196/2598434

94 Clayton, Paul, and Judith Rowbotham. "How the Mid-Victorians Worked, Ate and Died". *International Journal of Environmental Research and Public Health. (2009).*

95 https://www.plantnutritiontech.com/wp-content/uploads/2019/12/food_nutrition_decline.pdf

96 https://www.dailywire.com/news/yes-tariffs-are-still-stupid-heres-why-ben-shapiro

97 https://www.latimes.com/archives/la-xpm-1993-09-04-mn-31519-story.html

98 Chambers, *The Workshop of the World: British Economic history from 1820-1880,* 89

99 A full discussion can be found in: Hausmann & Hwang & Rodrik "What You Export Matters."

100 See: Porter, *The Competitive Advantage of Nations.*

101 Marchant, "An Overview of U.S. Foreign Direct Investment and Outsourcing," 286.

102 Ibid. 41.

103 Scott, "China, Trade, Outsourcing and Jobs," 18.

104 Defever & Riaño, "China's Pure Exporter Subsidies," 1.

105 Ibid. 7.

106 http://jasss.soc.surrey.ac.uk/16/3/7.html

107 Diamond. *Guns, Germs, and Steel.* p. 405

108 Lynn, Richard, & Tatu Vanhanen. *IQ and the Wealth of Nations.* p. xvi.

109 Ibid. 19.

110 Ibid. 107.

111 Ayres, "Technological Transformations and Long Waves," 16–17.

112 https://medium.com/parsa-vc/jumping-s-curves-building-a-high-performance-startup-80e4410466a5

113 Lynn & Vanhanen, p.98.

114 Dutton. *Genius Famine.* P.13

115 https://www.sciencedirect.com/science/article/abs/pii/S0160289612001286?via%3Dihub

116 https://nationalaffairs.com/publications/detail/the-disappearing-conservative-professor

117 https://www.aei.org/carpe-diem/more-evidence-that-its-really-hard-to-beat-the-market-over-time-95-of-finance-professionals-cant-do-it/

118 http://www.blackanddeckerappliances.com/products/cooking-appliances/toasters/4-slice-toaster-t4030.aspx

119 https://www.alibaba.com/product-detail/Black-Decker-Stainless-Steel-Toaster-with_60097392654.html?spm=a2700.7724857.normalList.2.51ae2970ApiQA0

120 http://www.globalsources.com/si/AS/Ningbo-East/6008849756690/pdtl/Black-Decker-Stainless-Steel-Toaster/1116113603.htm

121 Nicholas, *Medieval Flanders*, 290.

122 Nicholas, *Medieval Flanders*, 274.

123 Ibid. 279.

124 Fletcher, *Free Trade Doesn't Work: What should replace it and why*, 124.

125 Shepherd & Walton, The Economics of Early America, 71.

126 Wilson, *England's Apprenticeship, 1603-1763*. 185.

127 Chant & Gershman, "Kicking away the ladder: the "real" history of free trade by Ha-Joon Chang."

128 Shepherd & Walton, *Shipping, Maritime Trade and the Economic Development of Colonial North America*, 42.

129 Shepherd & Walton, *The Economics of Early America*, 72.

130 Ibid. 75.

131 Ibid. 77.

132 Shafaeddin, "How did developed countries industrialize? the history of trade and industrial policy: the cases of Great Britain and the USA" 3.

133 Ibid. 4.

134 Ibid.

135 Ayres, "Technological Transformations and Long Waves," 16-17.

136 Shafaeddin, "How did developed countries industrialize? the history of trade and industrial policy: the cases of Great Britain and the USA," 6.

137 Nye. "The Myth of Free-Trade Britain and Fortress France : Tariffs and Trade in the Nineteenth Century." 26 (Table 1).

138 Bairoch *Economics and World History: myths and paradoxes*, 47.

139 Ibid. 47.

140 Chambers, *The Workshop of the World: British Economic history from 1820–1880*, 118.

141 Ibid. 117.

142 Bairoch *Economics and World History: myths and paradoxes,* 51.

143 Mitchell & Deane. *Abstract of British Historical Statistics,* 520-21.

144 Chambers, *The Workshop of the World: British Economic history from 1820–1880*, 89.

145 Stebbins, *The American Protection's Manual*, 26.

146 https://www.brookings.edu/research/global-manufacturing-scorecard-how-the-us-compares-to-18-other-nations/ & https://www.bcg.com/en-ca

147 https://ourworldindata.org/grapher/historical-cost-of-computer-memory-and-storage?country=~OWID_WRL